SIMPLY DELICIOUS MEALS IN MINUTES

Simply Delicious Meals in Minutes

Darina Allen

Gill & Macmillan
Radio Telefís Éireann

For Timmy
who regularly rustles up memorable meals in minutes

Published by
Gill & Macmillan Ltd
Goldenbridge
Dublin 8
and
Radio Telefís Éireann
Donnybrook
Dublin 4
www.gillmacmillan.ie
© Darina Allen 1996
0 7171 2375 8

Photographs by Des Gaffney/RTE
Food styling by Rory O'Connell
Designed by Identikit Design Consultants, Dublin
Colour origination by Kulor Centre, Dublin
Printed by ColourBooks Ltd, Dublin

A catalogue record for this book is available from the British Library.

9   10   8

Contents

Preface...xi
Acknowledgments xiii
Glossary xv
Store Cupboard xvii

Soups

   Chicken, Avocado and Tomato Soup 2
^v Lebanese Cold Cucumber Soup......................................2
^v Persian Cocktail..3
   Potato and Sweetcorn Chowder 3
   Mushroom and Parsley Soup..4
   Courgette and Parsley Soup 5
   Pea and Coriander Soup 5
 * Chicken Noodle Soup 6
 * Cockle and Mussel Soup..7
   Tomato and Mint or Basil Soup....................................8
 * Tomato Soup with Pesto Crostini.................................9

Starters

 ^v Mozzarella, Tomato and Basil Salad............................10
^v* Traditional Greek Salad 11
   Popham's Avocado and Smoky Bacon Salad.............12
 * Thai Prawn Salad with Chilli and Fresh Coriander...................13
 ^v Lydia's Stuffed Mushrooms 13
^v* Guacamole with Salsa and Tortilla Chips..................14
 ^v Nachos with Tomato and Coriander Salsa.................15
^{vv} Chargrilled Red and Yellow Peppers 16

Meat 17

POULTRY

   Chicken Tikka with Poppodums and Tomato Relish.............18
 * Chicken Breasts with Gentle Spices.........................19
   Chicken Breasts with Thai Flavours 20

Chicken Goujons with Garlic Mayonnaise 20
* Pangrilled Chicken Breasts with Couscous, Raisins
   and Pistachio Nuts...21
Pangrilled Chicken Breasts with Rocket and
   Cherry Tomato Salad 22
Pangrilled Chicken Breasts with Corn Fritters
   and Crispy Bacon 23

LAMB

Moroccan Kebabs 23
Lamb Chops with Aubergine and Tomato Fondue...................24
Lamb's Liver with Sage Leaves 24
Lamb's Liver with Bacon 25
Lamb's Liver with Beetroot..25
Lamb's Kidneys with Grainy Mustard Sauce 26

BEEF

Steak with Mushroom à la Crème and Thyme Leaves 26
Elizabeth's Mustard Burgers 27
Stir-fried Beef with Crispy Vegetables and Oyster Sauce 28
* Mexican Mince with Tacos and Tomato Salsa...........................29
Spicy Indian Mince with Fluffy Rice 30
Chilli con Carne 31

PORK

Pork or Chicken with Mushrooms...33
Pork or Chicken with Mushrooms and Fresh Ginger 34
* Homemade Sausages with Bramley Apple Sauce and
   Scallion Champ 34
Homemade Sausages with Coriander 35
* Thai Stir-fried Pork with Ginger and Coriander........................35

Fish

* Goujons of Plaice, Sole or Monkfish with Various Sauces 37
   Thai Dipping Sauce 38
   Homemade Mayonnaise..39
   Garlic Mayonnaise 40
   Orly Sauce 40
   Quick Tartare Sauce 40
* Crispy Fish with Tartare Sauce..41

    * Fish and Chips 41
    Salmon with Tomato and Basil 42
    Salmon with Tomato and Fresh Parsley.................43
    Trout with Cream and Dill 43
    Pangrilled Fish with Flavoured Butters or Avocado Salsa 44
    * Mackerel Sandwich with Mushrooms and Fresh Herbs............46
    Fish in Paper Parcels with Hollandaise Sauce 47
    Papillote of Salmon with Tomato Concassé and Basil..............48
    Papillote of Salmon with Ginger Butter....................48
    Papillote of Salmon with Cucumber and Dill or Fennel 48
    Papillote of Salmon with Fresh Herbs.....................49
    Baked Cod Niçoise 49

Pasta

    * How to cook pasta..51
    V Spaghetti with Warm Tomato and Fresh Herb Sauce 51
    Spaghetti alla Carbonara..52
    Spaghetti alla Puttanesca.......................................53
    * Pasta Shells with Tomatoes, Spicy Sausage and Cream............53
    Pasta with Sardines, Pine Kernels and Raisins............54
    V Tagliatelle with Cream and Asparagus 55
    Tagliatelle with Smoked Salmon and Parsley 55
    V* Penne with Red and Yellow Peppers and Basil Leaves 56
    V Indian Spicy Noodles with Tomato.........................56
    V* Macaroni Cheese 57
    Macaroni Cheese with Smoked Salmon 58
    V Macaroni Cheese with Mushrooms and Courgettes..............58
    * Pasta Salad with Tuna and Beans.............................58
    V Orzo Salad with Pesto, Cherry Tomatoes and
        Knockalara Cheese 59
    V* Orzo with Pesto...60

Grains and Pulses

    V* How to boil rice to perfection...............................61
    * Pilaff Rice...62
    Pilaff with Fresh Herbs..62
    Pilaff with Mussels and Prawns...............................62
    * Fried Rice 63
    VV Couscous with Apricots and Toasted Almonds..............64
    VV* Tabouleh 64

vv Claudia Roden's Hummus bi Tahina 65

Lentils with Bacon 66

Egg and Cheese Dishes

v* Boiled Eggs with Soldiers and Asparagus 68

v* Perfect Poached Eggs on Toast................68

v* Buttered Eggs................69

v* Scrambled Eggs................69

* Scrambled Eggs with Smoked Salmon................70

v Scrambled Eggs with Tomato................70

v Scrambled Eggs with Tarragon and Basil 70

v Scrambled Eggs with Chives 70

v Scrambled Eggs with Asparagus................70

Scrambled Eggs with Smoked Bacon................70

v* Mexican Scrambled Eggs................71

v Indian Scrambled Eggs 71

v French Omelette................72

* Californian Omelette Sandwich 73

v* Frittata 74

Fluffy Savoury Omelette................75

v Ballymaloe Cheese Fondue 76

Pancakes, Crumpets and Fritters

Corn Fritters with Pangrilled Chicken Breasts

and Crispy Bacon 77

Toad in the Hole 78

v Pancakes 79

v Savoury Herb Pancakes................80

v Sweet Pancakes................80

Buttermilk Pancakes with Crispy Bacon and Maple Syrup........80

v Buttermilk Pancakes with Sour Cream and Jam................81

Buttermilk Pancakes with Crème Fraîche,

Dill and Smoked Salmon 81

v Drop Scones 81

Sandwiches and Breads

* Croissants with Ham, Mushrooms and Melted Cheddar Cheese..84

* Croissants with Crispy Bacon and Roasted Red Peppers 84

Chicken, Avocado and Mayonnaise with

Sundried Tomatoes in a Crusty Roll................85

Mussels, Avocado and Mayonnaise in a Crusty Roll..................85
v* Flat Mushroom Burgers with Pesto, Goat's Cheese
    and Sundried Tomatoes..86
v* Crawford Café Bruschetta..87
 * Quesadillas with Chicken and Salsa 87
v* Crunchy Tops...88
 v Focaccia with Red Onion, Olives and Rosemary.....................89
 v Panzerotte...90
 v Pizzette 91
 v French Toast with Bananas and Maple Syrup or Honey 91

Salads

vv A Good Green Salad with Various Dressings............................93
vv Greek Green Salad..94
   Caesar Salad...94
vv Pineapple, Cucumber and Mint Salad 95
   Thai Cucumber Salad 95
   Tuna Fish Salad...96

Vegetables

 v Buttered Cabbage 98
 v Cabbage with Caraway Seeds...98
   Cabbage with Crispy Bacon...98
vv Chinese Greens...98
 v Green Beans with Parmesan Cheese.....................................99
 v Frozen Peas with Fresh Mint...99
 v Grated Carrot with Sugar and Lemon 100
 v Stir-fried Vegetables..100
vv Tomato Fondue...101
 v Mushroom à la Crème 102
vv Piperonata...103
 v Aubergines with Various Toppings....................................103
vv Rustic Roasties...104
vv Crusty Peppered Potatoes...105
 v Scallion Champ..105
 v Hash Browns 106

Puddings

 v Plum and Almond Crumble 108
v* Banana Brulée..108

ᵛᵛ Fresh Fruit Salad of Peaches, Raspberries
and Melon with Mint 109
ᵛᵛ Sugared Peaches or Nectarines with
Fresh Raspberry Sauce 109
ᵛ Berry Fool 110
ᵛ Strawberry Shortcakes 110
ᵛ* Jane's Biscuits..111
ᵛ Vanilla Ice-cream with Delicious Sauces: Bitter Chocolate,
Toffee, Fresh Strawberry, Blackcurrant 111
ᵛ* Yoghurt with Honey and Toasted Hazelnuts..................113
ᵛ* Emily's Yoghurt Crunch 113
ᵛ* Hot Chocolate Soufflé 114
ᵛ Balloons 114
ᵛ Marianne's Almond Cake...115
ᵛ Barmbrack with Mascarpone 115
ᵛ Buttery Apple Croissants 116
ᵛ Apple and Cinnamon Fritters 116
ᵛ Banana Fritters 117
ᵛ Irish Blue Cheese with Honey 117

Index 118

* Recipes demonstrated on RTE's *Simply Delicious Meals
in Minutes* television series
ᵛ Recipes suitable for non-vegan vegetarians
ᵛᵛ Recipes suitable for vegans

Preface

For years, people have been asking me for a book and television series based on really fast recipes, so here it is at last. Every single thing in *Simply Delicious Meals in Minutes* can be cooked within half an hour, and indeed often in far less time than that. If I do nothing else, I'm determined to prove that it is perfectly possible to rustle up a delicious meal in the same time that it might take to reheat a ready-prepared dish from the supermarket.

There is no doubt that people have less and less time to spend in the kitchen. Even enthusiastic cooks often find themselves racing against the clock. In this kind of situation, a repertoire of fast, delicious and versatile dishes becomes an absolute necessity. This is something I have learnt myself, as my own life has become more and more hectic. Through experience, I have developed a survival kit which I am happy to pass on.

The first thing I have discovered is that it helps enormously to do a little advance planning. The busier you are, the more vital it becomes, so force yourself to sit down for half an hour and plan skeleton menus for the week ahead. This is the first step in a time and motion approach to cooking which enables you to achieve maximum return for minimum effort, both while shopping and in the kitchen. You will know what to buy when, and see how leftovers can be incorporated into meals later on in the week. Make your life easier by cooking double quantities when you can. It often takes the same cooking time and very little extra effort, and the benefit is that you have something in your fridge or freezer for the day when there isn't a minute to spare.

The other part of the equation is a well stocked store cupboard (see page xvii for suggestions). With a good combination of basics and a few small luxury items for the day when you are tired and weary, a comprehensive store cupboard means you need never be stuck. Although I always gravitate towards fresh foods in season, I'd be the first to admit that some very good things come in jars and tins. I have an undying passion for top-notch sardines in extra virgin olive oil, peppery gentleman's relish, Kalamati olives and sloe gin! Soy sauce, oyster sauce or my newest obsession, nam pla (fish sauce), can also add instant zizz to even the most mundane dishes.

Between my last series, *Simply Delicious Vegetables*, and this one, I have become even more fascinated by the flavours of the East and Mexico. Now, at last, it is possible to find the necessary ingredients in Ireland. Fresh chillies — the hottest thing sweeping across America and Europe — are widely available, as are fresh ginger and coriander. Even lemon grass, kaffir lime and fresh curry leaves are beginning to creep in. Ingredients like these, with spices from the store cupboard, can add magic to your cooking and make it easy to recreate wonderful dishes from cultures where exciting fast food is a way of life.

No matter what exotic ingredients may be to hand, however, for me the basis of quickly prepared meals will always be really good, fresh, local produce in season. Once again I exhort you to buy Irish and seek out the people in your own neighbourhood who are doing their best to produce natural foodstuffs of high quality. Support the family butchers, the organic and biodynamic growers, the farmhouse cheesemakers. It is a great reassurance to know where your food is coming from — and this will assume more importance as the trend towards processed food gathers momentum.

But back to the chopping board. Just because you are a busy, busy person, it doesn't mean you haven't the time to concoct something delicious to eat. There are well over a hundred recipes in this book alone to prove it — so have fun creating exciting meals in minutes.

Acknowledgments

I realise with astonishment that this is my eleventh book. As with the other ten, it would never have reached fruition without the support of a huge team of people, most of whom have been dedicated helpers in the past. They deserve not only my heartfelt thanks but admiration for submitting themselves to another round of frenzied effort to meet tight deadlines.

Special thanks are due to:

The Ballymaloe Cookery School team — secretaries Rosalie Dunne and Adrienne Morrissey; recipe testers Claire Cullinane, Pauline O'Driscoll, Sally O'Keefe, Rachel O'Neill.

The Gill & Macmillan publishing team — publisher Michael Gill; editors Mary Dowey, D Rennison Kunz.

The RTE television team — director and producer Colette Farmer; crew Kevin Cummins, Roy Bedell, Joe Kerins, Gary Finnegan, Pat Johns.

The food photography team — food stylist Rory O'Connell; photographers Des Gaffney, Denis O'Farrell.

My ever-encouraging family — Myrtle and Ivan Allen, Tim, Isaac, Toby, Lydia and Emily.

Glossary

Al dente: Firm to the bite.

Asafoetida: A powder with a strong aroma which is used primarily as an anti-flatulant. A little pinch added to beans while they are cooking enhances the flavour and makes them more socially acceptable!

Blanch: This cooking term can be confusing because it is used in many different senses. Usually it means to immerse food in water and to bring to the boil, parcook, extract salt or to loosen skins as in the case of almonds.

Deglaze: After meat has been sautéed or roasted, the pan or roasting dish is degreased and then a liquid is poured into the pan to dissolve the coagulated and caramelised pan juices. This is the basis of many sauces and gravies. The liquid could be water, stock or alcohol, e.g. wine or brandy.

Degrease: To remove surplus fat from a liquid or a pan, either by pouring off or by skimming the surface with a spoon.

Goujons: Narrow strips of fish or chicken cut across the grain. They are usually dipped in batter and deep-fried, but may also be coated in milk and seasoned flour, or cooked in flour, egg and crumbs.

Lardons: A French term for narrow strips of streaky bacon.

Nam Pla: A fish sauce made from fermented shrimps. A wonderful flavour enhancer which keeps for several months.

Pangrill: A heavy cast-iron pan, with a ridged bottom, either rounded or rectangular. The ridges mark the food attractively while keeping the meat or fish from direct contact with the fat. A heavy pan gives a good even heat.

Roux: Equal quantities of butter and flour cooked together for 2 minutes over a gentle heat. This mixture may be whisked into boiling liquid to thicken, e.g. gravies, sauces, milk etc. It can be kept in the fridge and used when needed.

Tomato Concassé: A term used to describe a small dice of peeled, ripe tomato flesh. Concassé may be added to a sauce or used as a garnish.

Measurements

All imperial spoon measurements in this book are rounded measurements unless the recipe states otherwise. All American spoon measurements are level.

Temperature Conversion

Approximate Fahrenheit/Centigrade equivalents are given in the recipes, but for fan or convection ovens it is wise to check the manufacturer's instructions regarding temperature conversion.

Store Cupboard

Busy people who want to be able to whizz up meals in minutes will need to ensure that their store cupboard is always well stocked. Here are some suggestions — all items I find invaluable.

Flour — *plain, self-raising, strong brown, strong white, coarse brown*

Oatmeal

Bread soda

Baking powder

Fast action dried yeast

Sugar — *white, dark brown, castor*

Dried fruit — *raisins, sultanas, mixed peel, apricots*

Ground almonds

Coconut

Cocoa

Vanilla essence

Pasta — *noodles, macaroni, shells, penne, spaghetti*

Grains — *couscous, bulgar*

Rice — *Basmati, Arborio, Thai fragrant*

Sardines

Tuna fish

Anchovies

Tinned sweetcorn

Tinned tomatoes

Olives (in oil rather than brine, or *olives à la grèque*)

Tinned beans — *flageolets, kidney beans, black-eyed beans, chick peas*

Lentils — *green, brown, Du Puy*

Stock cubes

Extra virgin olive oil

Groundnut oil

Sunflower oil

Red wine vinegar

White wine vinegar

English mustard powder

French mustard

Maldon sea salt

Black peppercorns

Harissa or chilli sauce

Some whole spices — *coriander, cardamom, nutmeg, cumin, cloves*

Nuts — *hazelnuts, walnuts, almonds*

Homemade jam

Irish honey

Marmalade

Tortillas

Tacos

Pitta bread

Cream crackers *or* **Carr's water biscuits**

Ballymaloe Tomato Relish

Ballymaloe Cucumber Pickle

Soy sauce (*preferably Kikkoman*)

Nam pla (*fish sauce*)

Oyster sauce

Plum sauce

Sesame oil

Fridge/cool larder

Butter

Buttermilk

Mature Cheddar cheese

Parmesan cheese

Eggs

Potatoes

Carrots

Onions

Garlic

Cooking apples

Lemons

A few treats

Gentleman's Relish

Panforte de Siena

Good chocolate (*e.g. Valrhona*)

Truffle oil

Balsamic vinegar

Maple syrup

Soups

Chicken, Avocado and Tomato Soup
^v Lebanese Cold Cucumber Soup
^v Persian Cocktail
Potato and Sweetcorn Chowder
Mushroom and Parsley Soup
Courgette and Parsley Soup
Pea and Coriander Soup
* Chicken Noodle Soup
* Cockle and Mussel Soup
Tomato and Mint or Basil Soup
* Tomato Soup with Pesto Crostini

You may wonder why there is a soup section in a book called *Simply Delicious Meals in Minutes*, but I have proved time and time again that it is perfectly possible to have fresh crusty bread (particularly scones) and a substantial homemade soup on the table within half an hour. The beauty of this is that it can be a complete meal — comforting, sustaining and inexpensive.

I promise you that all the soups in this section can easily be prepared within the 30-minute time limit.

However, it does make an enormous difference if you can use homemade stocks. Soups made with a base of really good, homemade stock will obviously be much more flavoursome than those made with water. (Stock cubes are a great stand-by, though obviously not quite the same as homemade stock.) The answer is to have some homemade stock 'in the bank'. On a day when you have time to spare, make a great big celebration pot of stock and freeze it in manageable lots.

Chicken, Avocado and Tomato Soup

T*his recipe came from my friend Mary Risley who runs an inspired cookery school called Tante Marie's in San Francisco.*

2 pints (1.2 L/5 cups) homemade
    chicken stock
1 chicken breast
1 ripe but firm avocado
2 ripe tomatoes, deseeded
    and diced
6 oz (170 g/1 generous cup)
    onion, finely chopped
1 tablespoon (1 generous
    American tablespoon)
    sunflower *or* arachide oil
2 cloves of garlic, finely chopped
3-4 dashes of Tabasco sauce
salt and freshly ground pepper
2 tablespoons approx.
    roughly chopped fresh
    coriander leaves
2 chillies, roasted, peeled
    and torn into strips
    (see method below)

Garnish
fresh coriander leaves
corn tortillas (optional)

Serves 6

Sweat the onion in the oil until soft and tender. Add the garlic and cook for another 1-2 minutes. Add the chicken stock and a few dashes of Tabasco sauce. Simmer for 5 minutes.

Meanwhile, skin the chicken breast if necessary. Cut the meat into ¼ inch (5 mm) strips. Season well with salt and freshly ground pepper. Add the chicken to the simmering broth and cook very gently until white all the way through.

Add the diced avocado and tomato flesh and simmer for another minute. Add the coarsely chopped coriander and the strips of diced roasted chillies (see below). Be careful not to overcook or the avocado will dissolve. Garnish with fresh coriander leaves and serve immediately.

To roast the chillies: Place them either over an open flame or under a grill until quite black. Put in a paper bag for 5 minutes. Peel off the black skin with your fingers and discard the seeds. Pull little strips for garnish.

Note: You could also add strips of corn tortillas to this soup if available. If fresh coriander is not available, use parsley. The soup will taste different but it will still be very good.

ᵛ Lebanese Cold Cucumber Soup

T*his is a cooling summer soup which can be made in almost the time it*

takes to grate the cucumber. If you haven't got time to chill the soup, pop the bowls

*into the freezer while you are making it.
Serve small portions because this soup
is rich.*

1 large crisp cucumber
8 fl oz (250 ml/1 cup) light cream
4 fl oz (120 ml/½ cup)
    natural yoghurt
2 tablespoons (2 generous
    American tablespoons)
    tarragon vinegar *or* white
    wine vinegar
½-1 clove of garlic, crushed
1 tablespoon approx. finely
    chopped gherkins

2 tablespoons approx. finely
    chopped fresh mint
salt and freshly ground pepper

Garnish
sprigs of mint

Serves 8

Grate the cucumber on the coarsest
part of the grater. Stir in all the other
ingredients. Season well. Serve chilled
in small bowls garnished with a sprig
of mint.

ᵛPersian Cocktail

This refreshing cocktail can be made in
minutes. *My mother-in-law brought
the recipe back from a trip to Persia just
before the fall of the Shah, hence the
name. Very ripe tomatoes are essential.*

8 oz (225 g) very ripe tomatoes
1 clove of garlic, peeled
    and crushed
1 level teaspoon salt
16 fl oz (475 ml/2 cups)
    natural yoghurt

1 teaspoon finely chopped
    fresh mint

Serves 6-8

Chop the tomatoes. Whizz in a food
processor or blender with the crushed
garlic and salt. Sieve out the tomato
skin and seeds, add the yoghurt, stir in
the mint and taste for seasoning. Serve
chilled in tall glasses.

Potato and Sweetcorn Chowder

A satisfying and filling soup made in a
short time. *This could be a supper
dish if eaten with a few scones and
followed by a salad.*

2-3 medium potatoes, parboiled
    for 10 minutes, drained,
    peeled and finely chopped

1 lb (450 g/2⅓ cups)
    sweetcorn kernels
1 oz (30 g/¼ stick) butter
6 oz (170 g/1 generous
    cup) approx. onion,
    finely chopped

10 fl oz (300 ml/1¼ cups)
   homemade chicken stock
10 fl oz (300 ml/1¼ cups) milk
salt and freshly ground pepper
8 fl oz (250 ml/1 cup) light
   cream *or* creamy milk

Garnish
roasted red pepper dice
   or crispy bacon dice
sprigs of flat parsley

Serves 4-6

Melt the butter in a heavy-bottomed saucepan, add the onion and potato and sweat until soft but not coloured. Gradually add in the stock and milk, stirring all the time, and bring to the boil. Simmer for a few minutes, add the corn, season with salt and freshly ground pepper, cover and cook gently for 10-15 minutes or until the potatoes are cooked. Add the cream and heat through gently without boiling.

Serve in hot bowls with a little dice of roasted red pepper or crispy bacon and parsley on top.

Note: If the soup is too thick, thin it out with a little chicken or vegetable stock.

Mushroom and Parsley Soup

T his is one of the fastest of all soups to make and surely everyone's favourite. Mushroom soup is best made with flat mushrooms or button mushrooms a few days old, which have developed a slightly stronger flavour. Here I have added a generous sprinkling of parsley to enhance the flavour even further.

1 lb (450 g/5 cups) mushrooms,
   finely chopped*
1½ oz (45 g/⅜ stick) butter
4 oz (110 g/scant 1 cup) onion,
   finely chopped
1 oz (30 g/scant ¼ cup) flour
salt and freshly ground pepper
1 pint (600 ml/2½ cups)
   homemade chicken stock
1 pint (600 ml/2½ cups) milk

1-2 tablespoons chopped
   fresh parsley
a dash of cream (optional)

Serves 8-9

Melt the butter in a saucepan on a gentle heat. Toss in the onion, cover and sweat until soft and completely cooked. Meanwhile, chop up the mushrooms very finely.* Add to the saucepan and cook on a high heat for 3-4 minutes.

Now stir in the flour, cook on a low heat for 2-3 minutes, season with salt and freshly ground pepper, then add the stock and milk gradually, stirring all the time. Increase the heat, add the parsley and bring to the boil. Taste, add a dash of cream if necessary and serve.

*If you can't be bothered to chop the mushrooms finely, just slice them and whizz the soup in a liquidiser for a few seconds when it is cooked.

Courgette and Parsley Soup

*C*hoose small courgettes for maximum flavour. If you are fortunate enough to grow your own, you'll have lots of bright yellow blossoms. Include some in the soup and scatter a few petals over each bowl of soup to make a stunning garnish.

1 lb (450 g) courgettes
1 oz (30 g/¼ stick) butter
6 oz (170 g 1¼ cups) onion, diced
6 oz (170 g/1 cup) potato, diced
salt, freshly ground pepper
    and nutmeg
1½ pints (900 ml/3¾ cups) light
    homemade chicken stock
2 tablespoons approx. chopped
    fresh parsley *or* 1 tablespoon
    approx. chopped fresh basil
    or annual marjoram
a dash of creamy milk
    (optional)

Serves 6-8

Melt the butter in a heavy-bottomed saucepan, add the onion and potato and toss until well coated. Season with salt, freshly ground pepper and nutmeg, cover and sweat until soft but not coloured — 5-6 minutes.

Meanwhile grate the courgettes on the coarse part of the grater and add to the soup base, stir and cook for 1-2 minutes. Bring the stock to the boil and add to the base, bring back to the boil and continue to cook for a further 4-5 minutes or until the vegetables are tender.

Add the parsley and purée the soup in a liquidiser for just a few seconds — there should be flecks of green clearly visible.

Taste and correct the seasoning. Add a little creamy milk if necessary.

Pea and Coriander Soup

*T*his utterly delicious soup has a perky zing with the addition of fresh chilli.

1 lb (450 g/4 cups) peas (good
    quality frozen are fine)
2 oz (55 g/½ stick) butter
5 oz (140 g/1 cup) onion,
    finely chopped
2 cloves of garlic, peeled
    and chopped

1 green chilli, deseeded and
    finely chopped
1½ pints (900 ml/3¾ cups)
    homemade chicken stock
2 tablespoons approx. chopped
    fresh coriander
salt, freshly ground pepper
    and sugar

Garnish
softly whipped cream
fresh coriander leaves

Serves 6 approx.

Melt the butter on a gentle heat and sweat the onion, garlic and chilli for 3-4 minutes. Add the peas and cover with the stock. Bring to the boil and simmer for 7-8 minutes.

Add the coriander and liquidise. Season with salt, freshly ground pepper and a pinch of sugar, which enhances the flavour even further.

Serve with a swirl of softly whipped cream and a few fresh coriander leaves sprinkled over the top.

*Chicken Noodle Soup

Since my trip to Wagamama, the Japanese noodle restaurant in London, we have been crazy about noodle soups. It must be said that my version bears little resemblance to the original — partly because mirin, bonita flakes and menma are not too easy to source in Shanagarry village! These soups are tremendously comforting without being too filling. Serve in large, shallow soup dishes.

4 oz (110 g) egg noodles
2½ pints (1.4 L/6¼ cups) homemade chicken stock
4 pints (2.3 L/10 cups) water
2 teaspoons salt
1 inch (2.5 cm) piece of fresh root ginger, sliced
1 large chicken breast — free-range if possible, skinless and boneless
2 generous tablespoons spring onion, green and white parts, cut into ½ inch (1 cm) lengths at an angle
1 green chilli, thinly sliced and finely chopped

6-8 tablespoons (8-10 American tablespoons) shredded iceberg lettuce
4 tablespoons (5 generous American tablespoons) chopped fresh coriander leaves
3-4 tablespoons (4-5 American tablespoons) soy sauce, *or* to taste (we use Kikkoman)
salt and freshly ground pepper

4 large wide soup bowls

Serves 4

Bring the water to a fast rolling boil, add the salt and then the noodles, stir well and continue to cook for 4 minutes. Drain. Bring the chicken stock slowly to the boil with the slices of fresh ginger. Slice the chicken breast very thinly across the grain. Prepare the iceberg lettuce, spring onion, chilli and coriander.

Add the chicken breast to the stock and simmer very gently for 2-3 minutes, add the noodles followed by the spring onion and chilli. Season well with salt and freshly ground pepper.

Fish out the slices of ginger if you wish and then put 2 tablespoons approx. of shredded lettuce into each bowl. Ladle the noodle soup over the top, add 1 tablespoon approx. of fresh coriander leaves to each bowl and season to taste with soy sauce. Eat immediately.

* Cockle and Mussel Soup

F ish soups can be a meal in themselves. Sweet cockles like the ones on Barrow strand in Co. Kerry can be found in several places around our coast, as can mussels, but it is vital that they be gathered from a clean source. If in doubt, buy shellfish from your fishmonger, in which case it will be purified. Mussels alone may be used if cockles are unavailable. Use this recipe as a base to utilise whatever fish and shellfish are available to you — a mixture would be great.

1½ lb (675 g) cockles
3½ lb (1.575 kg) mussels
4 tablespoons (5 generous American tablespoons) extra virgin olive oil
8 oz (225 g/1½ generous cups) onion, chopped
2 cloves of garlic
1 chilli, deseeded and finely chopped (optional)
¾ lb (350 g) very ripe tomatoes, peeled and chopped
5 fl oz (150 ml/generous ½ cup) dry white wine
1 pint (600 ml/2½ cups) water or fish stock (optional)

salt, freshly ground pepper and sugar
a dash of wine vinegar
1 teaspoon finely chopped fresh fennel
2 tablespoons approx. finely chopped fresh parsley or coriander

Serves 6 approx.

Heat the oil in a wide sauté pan, fry the onion and garlic on a gentle heat until golden, add the chopped chilli and tomatoes and continue to cook for 5-6 minutes. Add the wine, fish stock or water, salt, freshly ground pepper, a pinch of sugar and wine vinegar. Increase the heat, bring to the boil and cook for a further 10 minutes.

When you are ready to eat, pop a few deep, wide soup bowls into the oven. Add the cockles and mussels to the tomato base. As soon as the shells open, taste and correct the seasoning. Sprinkle the soup with fennel and parsley or fresh coriander. Ladle into the hot bowls and serve immediately with lots of crusty bread.

Tomato and Mint or Basil Soup

We worked for a long time to try and make this soup foolproof. Good quality tinned tomatoes (a must for your store cupboard) give a really good result. Homemade tomato purée, although delicious, can give a more variable result depending on the quality of the tomatoes.

2 × 14 oz (400 g) tins of tomatoes,
    liquidised and sieved,
    + 2 teaspoons sugar
1 small onion, finely chopped
½ oz (15 g/⅛ stick) butter
8 fl oz (250 ml/1 cup) Béchamel
    sauce (see below)
8 fl oz (250 ml/1 cup) homemade
    chicken *or* vegetable stock
2 tablespoons approx. chopped
    fresh mint *or* basil
salt, freshly ground pepper
    and sugar
4 fl oz (120 ml/½ cup)
    cream (optional)

Garnish
fresh mint *or* basil leaves

Serves 6

Sweat the onion in butter on a gentle heat until soft but not coloured. Add the tomatoes, Béchamel sauce and homemade stock. Add the chopped mint or basil. Season with salt, freshly ground pepper and sugar. Bring to the boil and simmer for a few minutes. Liquidise, taste, and dilute further with stock if necessary. Bring back to the boil, correct the seasoning, and add a little cream if you fancy. Serve in hot soup bowls garnished with fresh mint or basil leaves.

Note: This soup needs to be tasted carefully as the final result depends on the quality of the tomato purée, stock etc. Sugar is essential to counteract the acidity of tinned tomatoes.

QUICK BÉCHAMEL SAUCE

½ pint (300 ml/1¼ cups) milk
1½ oz (45 g/scant ⅓ cup) roux
    (see glossary)
salt and freshly ground pepper

This is a wonderfully quick way of making Béchamel sauce if you have roux already made. Put the cold milk into a saucepan and bring to the boil. Whisk in roux until the sauce is of a light coating consistency. Season with salt and freshly ground pepper and allow to bubble on a low heat for a few minutes. Taste and correct the seasoning if necessary.

* TOMATO SOUP WITH PESTO CROSTINI

Pesto (see page 60)
6 crostini made from ¼ inch
    (5 mm) thick slices of French
    bread, toasted or cooked in
    olive oil until crisp and
    pale golden

Omit the mint or basil from the soup recipe.

To serve, spread a little blob of Pesto on 6 freshly cooked crostini and drop one into each bowl just before serving.

Starters

v **Mozzarella, Tomato and Basil Salad**
v* **Traditional Greek Salad**
Popham's Avocado and Smoky Bacon Salad
* **Thai Prawn Salad with Chilli and Fresh Coriander**
v **Lydia's Stuffed Mushrooms**
v* **Guacamole with Salsa and Tortilla Chips**
v **Nachos with Tomato and Coriander Salsa**
vv **Chargrilled Red and Yellow Peppers**

When time is of the essence, starters, sadly, are often the part of the meal most likely to be jettisoned. A pity, because they can be light and tantalising and set the mood for a delicious meal which doesn't have to be very elaborate. In fact, I often enjoy a meal of several starters far more than just one conventional main course. There is a general trend away from the traditional meat and two veg towards smaller, lighter dishes. No doubt the reason is that these leave people feeling satisfied, rather than uncomfortably bloated.

All of these starters are quick to prepare and terrifically tasty.

v Mozzarella, Tomato and Basil Salad

The success of this summery salad depends on the quality of the Mozzarella. Don't attempt it with the bland, slightly rubbery Mozzarella which comes in large slabs. The little rounds of buffalo Mozzarella sold vacuum-packed in their whey are becoming more widely available, so seek them out. Although never quite as meltingly tender as the Fior Mozzarella di Buffalo that you will find around Naples in Southern Italy, they can still be very delicious.

6 oz (170 g) buffalo
    Mozzarella cheese
10 oz (285 g) firm,
    ripe tomatoes
sea salt, freshly cracked
    pepper and sugar
lots of fresh basil
4 tablespoons (5 American
    tablespoons) extra virgin
    olive oil *or* Basil Dressing
    (see opposite)

Garnish
a few fresh basil leaves

Accompaniment
crusty bread *or* Focaccia

Serves 4

Slice the tomatoes ¼ inch (5 mm) thick. Season with sea salt, plenty of freshly cracked pepper and a little sugar. Add a few torn basil leaves and toss gently, then drizzle generously with the extra virgin olive oil or Basil Dressing.

Carefully slice the Mozzarella into ¼ inch (5 mm) thick rounds, (really good Mozzarella is tender and delicate). Put one or two pieces of Mozzarella on a white plate and place a few pieces of tomato haphazardly

alongside. Drizzle the Mozzarella with oil or Basil Dressing. Garnish with a few leaves of basil and a sprinkle of freshly cracked pepper. Serve with lots of crusty country bread or Focaccia.

BASIL DRESSING
24 fl oz (700 ml/3 cups) good quality extra virgin olive oil
8 fl oz (250 ml/1 cup) white wine vinegar
salt, freshly ground pepper and sugar
4 cloves of garlic
1 large bunch (1 loosely packed cup) fresh basil

Liquidise all the ingredients and store in a screw-top jar.

ᵛ* Traditional Greek Salad

T his salad is served in virtually every *taverna in Greece and is delicious when made with really fresh ingredients and eaten immediately. We use our local Knockalara ewe's milk cheese instead of Feta which is seldom in the condition that the Greeks intended by the time it reaches us!*

⅓-½ crisp cucumber
6 very ripe tomatoes
6 scallions
12-18 Kalamati olives
2 tablespoons approx. chopped fresh annual marjoram

extra virgin olive oil
freshly squeezed lemon juice
salt, freshly cracked pepper and sugar
2-3 oz (55-85 g) cubed Knockalara ewe's milk cheese* *or* fresh Feta
sprigs of flat parsley

Serves 6

Halve the cucumber lengthwise and cut into chunks. Chop coarsely the green and white parts of the scallions. Core the tomatoes and cut into wedges. Mix the tomatoes, cucumber, scallion, olives and marjoram in a bowl, and sprinkle with olive oil and lemon juice. Season with salt, freshly cracked pepper and sugar and toss well. Sprinkle with ½ inch (1 cm) cubes of cheese and sprigs of flat parsley.

Serve at once.

Note: Slices of red pepper may be included.

*Knockalara cheese, Cappoquin, Co. Waterford, Tel. (024) 96326.

Popham's Avocado and Smoky Bacon Salad

Popham's is a delightful little restaurant with just one table in the village of Winkleigh in the south of England. It is owned and run by the irrepressible Melvyn Popham and Denis Hawkes and is certainly 'worth a detour'.

2 avocados

6-8 thin slices smoky bacon, cut into ¼ inch (5 mm) strips

a mixture of assorted salad leaves — radicchio, frisée, oakleaf, iceberg

2 tablespoons approx. tomato concassé (optional — see glossary)

salt, freshly ground pepper and sugar

12 seedless green grapes, halved

Dressing

2 tablespoons walnut oil

1 tablespoon extra virgin olive oil

salt and freshly ground pepper

Garnish

sprigs of fresh parsley *or* chervil

Serves 4

First make the dressing by whisking the ingredients together. Cut the avocado in half, remove the stone and then cut into quarters and cubes. Cut the bacon into lardons and cook in a little oil until crisp and golden.

Make the tomato concassé, season with salt, freshly ground pepper and sugar.

Toss the salad leaves in most of the dressing, divide between four plates and sprinkle with grape halves. Season the avocado and spoon on top. Sprinkle the sizzling streaky bacon over the avocado. Top with a little tomato concassé, drizzle a bit more dressing, garnish with sprigs of parsley or chervil and serve immediately.

*Thai Prawn Salad with Chilli and Fresh Coriander

*T*hai food can be an amazing taste sensation — a delight both for the eyes and palate with its contrasting hot, sweet, sour and salty flavours. Nam pla, as Thai fish sauce is known, is an essential ingredient in this recipe and a marvellous new addition to your store cupboard. Splash it into meat as well as fish dishes. You can obtain it, and other eastern ingredients such as lemon grass and fresh coriander, from the following places: the Asia market, Drury Street, Dublin 2, Tel. (01) 677 9764; Mr Bell, Old English Market, Cork, Tel. (021) 885333; and other speciality shops and some supermarkets around the country. Coriander is also extremely easy to grow from a packet of seed.

2 lb (900 g) fresh Tiger prawns, shrimps *or* Dublin bay prawns, cooked and shelled iceberg lettuce

CHILLI AND CORIANDER DRESSING
1 fresh red chilli
2 tablespoons approx. chopped fresh coriander
1 stem lemon grass
2 fl oz (50 ml/¼ cup) nam pla (fish sauce)

3 fl oz (75 ml/⅓ cup) freshly squeezed lemon juice
2 fl oz (50 ml/¼ cup) dry white wine
1 tablespoon (1 generous American tablespoon) soft brown sugar

Garnish
sprigs of fresh coriander

Serves 8 as a starter

First make the dressing. Roll the chilli, slice off the top, shake out the seeds and chop the flesh finely. Peel the outer leaves from the lemon grass, chop finely and mix with the chilli, chopped coriander and all the other ingredients, in a bowl.

Put the freshly cooked peeled prawns into the dressing, cover and marinate in the fridge for at least 30 minutes (1-2 hours would be even better).

Serve on a bed of shredded iceberg lettuce with some dressing spooned over the top. Garnish with sprigs of fresh coriander.

ᵛLydia's Stuffed Mushrooms

*M*y daughter Lydia pokes through the larder and fridge and then nonchalantly flings together all sorts of seemingly miscellaneous ingredients to make some delicious concoctions. This one was a triumph and has become a real favourite.

8 large flat mushrooms
1½ oz (45 g) pine kernels
½ lb (225 g/1 cup) Ricotta *or*
cottage cheese
2 oz (55 g/½ cup) freshly grated
Parmesan cheese (Parmigiano
Reggiano if possible)
2 teaspoons Pesto (see page 60)
salt and freshly ground pepper
8 Crostini (see below) *or* rounds
of hot toast

Serves 8

Preheat the oven to
230°C/450°F/regulo 8. Toast the
pine kernels in a hot oven or under a
grill. They burn really easily so keep a
good eye on them. Cool.

Mix the Ricotta or cottage
cheese, grated Parmesan and Pesto
together in a bowl. Season with salt
and freshly ground pepper. Fold in
the pine kernels. Taste. Season the
flat mushrooms with salt and freshly
ground pepper and divide the cheese
mixture between the mushrooms.

Put on to a baking tray, drizzle
with olive oil and cook until they
smell good — 15 minutes approx.
Serve each on a warm Crostini or a
round of hot toast. Eat and enjoy!

CROSTINI
8 rounds of good quality Italian
***or* French bread**
extra virgin olive oil

Heat 1 inch (2.5 cm) of olive oil in a
pan. When hot but not smoking,
drop in a few slices of bread; they will
turn golden in a few seconds. Turn
with tongs and cook until pale golden
on the other side. Remove from the
oil and drain on kitchen paper.
Repeat until all the Crostini are
cooked. Serve warm. Strain the oil
and save for another use.

ᵛ* Guacamole with Salsa and Tortilla Chips

For me *Mexican food is utterly
irresistible — as, indeed, are all
things Mexican. Tortilla chips are even
making their way into small supermarkets
and newsagents.*

1 ripe avocado
1 clove of garlic, crushed
(optional)
1-2 tablespoons (1-2 generous
American tablespoons) freshly
squeezed lime *or* lemon juice
1 tablespoon (1 generous
American tablespoon) extra
virgin olive oil
1 tablespoon (1 generous
American tablespoon)
chopped fresh coriander
***or* parsley**
sea salt and freshly ground pepper

Tomato and Coriander Salsa
(see page 29)
tortilla chips

Lebanese Cold Cucumber Soup

Persian Cocktail

Courgette and Parsley Soup

Chicken Goujons with Garlic Mayonnaise

Pangrilled Chicken Breasts with Rocket and Cherry Tomato Salad

Serves 4-6 as a starter

First make the Guacamole. Scoop out the flesh from the avocado. Mash with a fork, then add the crushed garlic, lime or lemon juice, olive oil, chopped coriander or parsley, salt and freshly ground pepper to taste.

Next make the Tomato and Coriander Salsa. To serve, put a generous tablespoon of Tomato and Coriander Salsa into one bowl and a good blob of Guacamole into another. Put on to a plate, add lots of crisp Tortilla chips for dipping and serve immediately. Quite simply, addictive!

ʼNachos with Tomato and Coriander Salsa

N *achos are becoming all the rage as enthusiasm for Mexican food gathers momentum, and it becomes easier and easier to find the ingredients in supermarkets and delicatessens. The chillies heat and the Mozzarella cheese cools.*

8 tortillas (corn tortillas are more authentic but wheat flour tortillas will still be delicious)
oil for frying
salt
2-3 green chillies, finely sliced
4 oz (110 g/1 cup) buffalo Mozzarella cheese, grated
or
2 oz (55 g/½ cup) Mozzarella, grated and 2 oz (55 g/½ cup) mature Irish Cheddar cheese, grated

Accompaniment
Tomato and Coriander Salsa (see page 29)

Serves 4 as a starter or more for compulsive nibbling

Cut the tortillas into quarters or sixths. Heat some oil; a deep-frier is easiest but you can manage in a frying pan. The oil should be hot — 200°C/400°F. Fry the pieces until pale golden, remove with a slotted spoon, drain on kitchen paper and sprinkle with salt.

Add some sliced chilli to each one and top with a little grated cheese. Flash under a grill or pop into a hot oven until the cheese melts. Serve immediately with Tomato and Coriander Salsa.

Allow about 8 Nachos per person as a starter. They also make a great appetiser accompanied with a tomato salad.

^{vv} Chargrilled Red and Yellow Peppers

The sweet, slightly smoky flavour of roast or chargrilled peppers has become one of the hottest new favourites as the craze for Mediterranean food continues unabated. Every now and then I roast lots of peppers and store them peeled and seeded in a glass Kilner jar with a few fresh basil leaves and lots of extra virgin olive oil. They are extremely useful in toppings, salads or as a delicious accompaniment to pangrilled fish, meat, lentils or goat cheese. Here they star in their own right.

**8 fleshy red and yellow peppers
(Italian *or* Spanish if possible)
8 fresh basil leaves
extra virgin olive oil
10-12 black Kalamati olives
(optional)
sea salt and freshly cracked
pepper
rocket leaves (optional)**

Accompaniment
**crusty bread *or* Ciabatta
or Focaccia**

Serves 8

Preheat the grill or better still use a charcoal grill or barbecue. Grill the peppers on all sides, turning them when necessary — they can be quite charred. Alternatively, preheat the oven to 250°C/475°F/regulo 9. Put the peppers on a baking tray and bake for 20-30 minutes until the skin blisters and the flesh is soft.

Put them into a bowl and cover with cling film for a few minutes — this will make them much easier to peel.

Pull the skin off the peppers, remove the stalks and seeds. Do not wash or you will lose the precious sweet juices. Divide each into 2 or 3 pieces along the natural divisions.

Arrange the peeled peppers with colours alternating on a wide serving dish. Season with sea salt and freshly cracked pepper and drizzle with extra virgin olive oil. Scatter a few black olives and some rocket or basil leaves over the top if liked. Serve with crusty white bread, Ciabatta or Focaccia.

Meat

Poultry recipes, pages 18-23
Lamb recipes, pages 23-26
Beef recipes, pages 26-32
Pork recipes, pages 33-36

For busy people, cooking in a hurry generally means buying the more expensive cuts of meat — steak, lamb cutlets, chicken breasts, pork fillet — because these withstand fast cooking methods best. If you are taking this short cut, it is more important than ever to seek out a reliable local butcher who knows his sources and can be depended upon to provide naturally reared meat of the highest quality.

Stewing meat is pretty much out of the question because it will be like old shoe leather without the long, slow cooking it needs, but wonderfully tasty dishes can be made quickly from mince — the cheapest meat of all.

One of the compensations for having a library of cookbooks which is fast threatening to engulf me is that I can quickly discover how other cultures treat universally available foodstuffs. As I flicked through the pages of some books recently, my ways of cooking mince suddenly began to seem exceedingly boring. It was a revelation to find so many other exciting possibilities. In Mexico mince is zapped up with lots of chilli and coriander, and served with tortillas. In India it is enlivened with wonderful fresh spices and served with a creamy yoghurt raita and paratha or naan bread.

The East is a rich source of inspiration for anybody who needs to cook really tasty meat dishes in minutes. After all, Indian, Chinese and Thai cooks are the masters of genuinely exciting fast food. They have also perfected the art of making a few tasty morsels of meat go a very long way. A skill worth acquiring!

POULTRY

Chicken Tikka with Poppodums and Tomato Relish
* *Chicken Breasts with Gentle Spices*
Chicken Breasts with Thai Flavours
Chicken Goujons with Garlic Mayonnaise
* *Pangrilled Chicken Breasts with Couscous,*
Raisins and Pistachio Nuts
Pangrilled Chicken Breasts with Rocket
and Cherry Tomato Salad
Pangrilled Chicken Breasts with Corn Fritters
and Crispy Bacon

Chicken Tikka with Poppodums and Tomato Relish

T hese are exceedingly good either hot or cold. Try eating the chicken breasts in a crusty Ciabatta sandwich with Spicy Tomato Mayonnaise (see page 21).

6 × 4 oz (110 g) chicken breasts —
   free-range if possible,
   skinless and boneless
2 teaspoons ground cumin seeds
2 teaspoons paprika
¾ teaspoon cayenne pepper
2 teaspoons ground turmeric
½ teaspoon freshly ground
   black pepper
1 teaspoon salt
2 small cloves of garlic, crushed
2½ tablespoons approx. freshly
   squeezed lemon juice
1–2 tablespoons approx.
   sunflower oil

Accompaniments
Ballymaloe Tomato Relish
   (available in delicatessens
   countrywide)
sliced bananas, sprinkled
   with lemon juice
6 poppodums

Serves 6

   Cut the chicken breasts into large cubes.
   Mix the cumin, paprika, cayenne, turmeric, black pepper, salt, garlic and lemon juice in a bowl. Rub this mixture all over the chicken pieces, put in the bowl, cover and refrigerate or keep in a cool place for as long as you can spare.
   Preheat the oven to 200°C/400°F/regulo 6. Put the chicken pieces on to a roasting tin with all the paste. Brush or drizzle

with a little oil and bake for 10 minutes approx., then turn over and bake for a further 10-15 minutes depending on the size of the pieces. Baste two or three times during cooking.

Meanwhile, cook the poppodums following the instructions on the packet.

Transfer the chicken to a serving dish, spoon the degreased juices (see glossary) over the chicken and serve hot or lukewarm with Ballymaloe Tomato Relish, some sliced bananas and the poppodums.

*Chicken Breasts with Gentle Spices

E*ven determined curry haters have enjoyed this deliciously spiced recipe.*

4-6 chicken breasts — free-range if possible, skinless and boneless
1 heaped teaspoon whole cardamom pods
1 heaped teaspoon whole coriander seeds
1 heaped teaspoon whole cumin seeds
1 oz (30 g/¼ stick) butter
4 oz (110 g/scant 1 cup) onion, chopped
salt and freshly ground pepper
¼ pint (150 ml/generous ½ cup) homemade chicken stock
¼ pint (150 ml/generous ½ cup) cream

Garnish
fresh flat parsley or coriander

Accompaniment
Fluffy Rice (see page 31) or Orzo (see page 59)

Serves 4-6

Press the cardamom pods to extract the seeds, and discard the pods. Grind to a fine powder with the coriander and cumin seeds, with a pestle and mortar or in a spice grinder.

Melt the butter in a sauté pan, add the onion and sweat over a gentle heat until soft. Season the chicken with salt and freshly ground pepper, rub in the ground spices, add the chicken to the onion and sauté gently without browning for 2-3 minutes. Turn each piece so that it is sealed all over. Add the chicken stock, cover the pan tightly and cook on a gentle heat for 8-10 minutes or until the chicken pieces are cooked but still nice and juicy.

Remove the chicken to a serving dish and keep warm. Put the casserole back on the heat, add the cream and reduce by half. Taste and adjust the seasoning, add the chicken pieces back into the sauce, allow to bubble for 1-2 minutes, then arrange in a warm serving dish. Garnish with flat parsley or coriander and serve with Fluffy Rice or Orzo.

Chicken Breasts with Thai Flavours

T*hai food with its contrasting hot, sweet, sour and salty flavours is taking Europe and The United States by storm. This is yet another way of injecting life into bland chicken breasts.*

**6 chicken breasts — free-range
    if possible, skinless
    and boneless**
oil

Marinade
2 tablespoons approx. sesame oil
2 cloves of garlic, crushed
**1 teaspoon chopped fresh
    coriander (both top and stalk)**
**1 fresh red chilli, deeeded and
    finely chopped**
**2 tablespoons approx. nam pla
    (fish sauce)**
1 teaspoon sugar

Thai Sauce
**6 tablespoons (8 American
    tablespoons) rice wine vinegar**
**3 tablespoons (4 American
    tablespoons) sugar**
½ teaspoon salt
2 cloves of garlic, crushed

**1 tablespoon approx. chopped
    fresh coriander**
**3 red chillies, deseeded and
    finely chopped**

Garnish
sprigs of coriander

Serves 6

Mix all the ingredients for the marinade in a pie dish, turn the chicken breasts in it and leave them to absorb the flavours while you make the sauce.

Put the vinegar into a small stainless steel saucepan over a low heat, add the sugar and stir until it has dissolved. Add the salt and simmer 3-4 minutes or until the liquid thickens slightly. Allow to cool. Add the crushed garlic, coriander and chillies and put into a serving bowl.

Preheat a grill or pangrill. Drain the chicken breasts, brush with oil and cook for approx. 4 minutes on each side or until cooked through but still tender and juicy. Garnish with sprigs of fresh coriander and serve immediately with the Thai Sauce.

Chicken Goujons with Garlic Mayonnaise

T*his is a clever, quick and delicious way to make a little chicken go a long way.*

**2-3 chicken breasts — free-range
    if possible, skinless
    and boneless**
salt and freshly ground pepper

batter (see page 38) *or* seasoned
flour, beaten egg and
breadcrumbs *or* milk and
seasoned flour
good quality oil for deep-frying
Garlic Mayonnaise (see page 40)
or Chilli and Parsley
Mayonnaise (see below) *or*
Spicy Tomato Mayonnaise
(see below)

Heat the oil in a deep-frier. Cut the
chicken breasts into ½ inch (1 cm)
strips on the bias. Season with salt
and freshly ground pepper, dip in
batter or flour, egg and breadcrumbs,
or simply in milk and seasoned flour.
Drop individually into the batter
and fry for 2–3 minutes or until crisp
and golden.

Drain on kitchen paper. Serve
immediately on a hot plate with a

blob or bowl of well seasoned
mayonnaise of your choice.

GOUJONS AND CHIPS
Goujons mixed with crispy chips,
piled high on a plate, are also
delicious. Dip both chips and goujons
in the sauce or sauces of your choice.

CHILLI AND PARSLEY MAYONNAISE
Add 1 roasted, peeled, deseeded
and chopped fresh chilli and 2
tablespoons of chopped parsley
to one quantity of Homemade
Mayonnaise (see page 39).

SPICY TOMATO MAYONNAISE
Stir a generous tablespoon of
Ballymaloe Country Relish into one
quantity of the Homemade
Mayonnaise recipe on page 39.

*Pangrilled Chicken Breasts with Couscous, Raisins and Pistachio Nuts

Hot, peppery Harissa smeared over the pangrilled chicken breasts adds even more excitement!

8 chicken breasts — free-range if
possible, skinless and boneless
1 pint (600 ml/2½ cups) well
flavoured chicken stock
12 oz (340 g/3 cups) couscous
4 oz (110 g/¾ cup) raisins
1½ oz (45 g/½ cup) toasted split
almonds *or* 1½ oz (45 g/½
cup) pistachio nuts
salt and freshly ground pepper

4 tablespoons (5 American
tablespoons) extra virgin
olive oil
a little butter *or* extra virgin olive
oil (optional)
Harissa (hot chilli paste —
optional)

Garnish
sprigs of coriander

Serves 8

Cover the couscous in its own
volume of chicken stock or water

(16 fl oz/475 ml/scant 2 cups) and allow to soak for 15 minutes, stirring every now and then. When the liquid has been absorbed, add the raisins and toasted almonds or pistachio nuts, and season with salt and freshly ground pepper. Put into a thick covered dish and heat through in a preheated moderate oven at 180°C/350°F/regulo 4 for 20 minutes approx.

Season the chicken breasts with salt and freshly ground pepper. Brush with the olive oil and cook on a preheated pangrill until just cooked through and golden on both sides.

To serve, turn the couscous into a hot serving dish, add butter or olive oil to taste, and season with salt and freshly ground pepper. Spread a little Harissa, if using, on the pangrilled chicken breasts. Arrange them on top of the couscous. Degrease the grill pan and deglaze with a little well flavoured chicken stock.

Garnish with sprigs of fresh coriander and serve immediately.

Pangrilled Chicken Breasts with Rocket and Cherry Tomato Salad

4 chicken breasts — free-range if possible, skinless and boneless
1-2 tablespoons approx. olive oil

Rocket and Cherry Tomato Salad (see below)

Serves 4

Heat a cast-iron grill pan until quite hot. Remove the fillet from each chicken breast to cook separately or keep for a stir-fry. The chicken breast will now cook more evenly. Brush each chicken breast with oil and season with salt and freshly ground pepper. Place the chicken breasts on the hot pangrill and allow to become golden brown on both sides, turning several times to get nice grill marks. They will take 10-15 minutes to cook depending on size.

Serve with Rocket and Cherry Tomato Salad.

ROCKET AND CHERRY TOMATO SALAD
4 fistfuls of rocket *or* equivalent of mixed salad leaves
8-10 cherry tomatoes — red and yellow if possible
salt, freshly ground pepper and sugar
a little chopped fresh mint *or* basil (optional)

Basic French Dressing (see page 93)

Cut the tomatoes in half and season with salt, freshly ground pepper, sugar and a little chopped fresh mint or basil if available. Toss the rocket leaves with salad dressing and scatter the cherry tomatoes over the top.

PANGRILLED CHICKEN BREASTS WITH CORN FRITTERS AND CRISPY BACON

S ee page 77.

LAMB

Moroccan Kebabs
Lamb Chops with Aubergine and Tomato Fondue
Lamb's Liver with Sage Leaves
Lamb's Liver with Bacon
Lamb's Liver with Beetroot
Lamb's Kidneys with Grainy Mustard Sauce

Moroccan Kebabs

G *reat for a barbecue, these delicious spicy kebabs can also be cooked under a grill or on a pangrill. I sometimes intersperse the meat with little cubes of dried apricot.*

2 lb (900 g) lean lamb — leg meat cut into 1 inch (2.5 cm) cubes
1 tablespoon (1 generous American tablespoon) cumin seeds
1 teaspoon ground turmeric

2 teaspoons fresh root ginger, grated
1 teaspoon freshly cracked black peppercorns
1 teaspoon chopped fresh parsley
finely chopped shallot *or* small spring onion
1 clove of garlic, crushed
sea salt

Serves 6-8

Heat the cumin seeds on a pan for a few seconds, then grind or pound with a pestle and mortar. Mix with the other spices and add the parsley, onion and garlic. Mix with the meat and leave in a covered bowl for at least 30 minutes (1-2 hours would be better still). Thread on to flat skewers. Grill on a medium heat for 8-10 minutes.

Serve immediately with Couscous (see page 64) and Ballymaloe Tomato Relish, available in most good food shops.

Lamb Chops with Aubergine and Tomato Fondue

*T*his is a delicious combination. *Although aubergines are initially an acquired taste, they soon become addictive!*

8 centre- or sideloin lamb chops
1 aubergine
salt and freshly ground pepper
plenty of extra virgin olive oil

Tomato Fondue (see page 101)
Pesto (optional — see page 60)

Garnish
sprigs of mint

Serves 4

Slice the aubergine into rounds ½ inch (1 cm) thick — you'll need 8 slices at least. If you have time, sprinkle with salt and allow to degorge, then dry with kitchen paper. This is far from essential, however: I usually go right ahead and fry the aubergines.

Heat a pangrill. Season the lamb chops with salt and freshly ground pepper and cook to your taste on both sides.

Heat 1 inch (2.5 cm) of olive oil in a frying pan. (Don't worry about wasting so much — the oil may be used again for another purpose.) Cook the aubergines in the hot oil until a rich golden brown on each side. Drain on a wire rack over a baking sheet.

Heat the Tomato Fondue. Arrange the lamb chops on a hot serving dish surrounded with aubergine slices, top each slice with a spoonful of hot Tomato Fondue and a blob of Pesto. Garnish with sprigs of mint and serve immediately.

Lamb's Liver with Sage Leaves

*T*he robust flavour of sage is just great *with lamb's liver, so be sure to keep a sage plant in a pot near your kitchen door.*

Sage leaves crisped in olive oil make an irresistible garnish.

1 lb (450 g) very fresh spring
   lamb's liver, cut in ½ inch
   (1 cm) slices
a little seasoned white flour
2 tablespoons extra virgin olive oil
12-16 fresh sage leaves

Serves 4

Toss the liver in seasoned flour and
pat off the excess. Heat half the olive
oil in a frying pan and add the liver.
Sauté gently for 2-3 minutes on each
side and remove the slices while they
are still slightly pink in the centre.
Put the remaining olive oil in the
pan, add the sage leaves and allow to
sizzle for a few seconds until crisp.
Pour the oil, juices and sage leaves
over the liver and serve immediately.
Even if liver is perfectly cooked, it
toughens very quickly if kept hot.

Lamb's Liver with Bacon

C ook two slices of streaky bacon
per person until crisp and golden.
Cook the liver gently as above. Serve
immediately on hot plates with the
crispy bacon on top.

Lamb's Liver with Beetroot

A *listair Little introduced me to this
delicious combination.*

1 lb (450 g) spring lamb's liver,
   cut in ½ inch (1 cm) slices
seasoned flour
½ oz (15 g/⅛ stick) butter
1 lb (450 g) cooked baby beetroot
16 fl oz (475 ml/2 cups)
   homemade chicken stock
5 fl oz (150 ml/generous ½ cup)
   cream
salt and freshly ground pepper
a squeeze of fresh lemon juice

Garnish
coarsely chopped parsley

Serves 4

Cut the beetroot into ¼ inch (5 mm)
thick batons. Toss the liver in well
seasoned flour. Melt the butter in a
hot frying pan, and as soon as it foams
add the liver in a single layer. Seal
quickly on one side, then on the
other. Transfer to a plate. Deglaze the
pan with stock, boil for 1-2 minutes,
add the cream and beetroot, and
allow to bubble for a few minutes
until the beetroot heats through.
Taste and add a squeeze of lemon
juice if necessary. Return the liver to
the pan and simmer for 1-2 minutes.
Sprinkle with parsley and serve
immediately on hot plates.

Lamb's Kidneys with Grainy Mustard Sauce

I adore kidneys and can't understand why they are not more sought after. They are usually ridiculously cheap and are best cooked very quickly.

8 lamb's kidneys (still in suet
   if possible)
a little butter
salt and freshly ground pepper
   to taste
2 tablespoons (2½ American
   tablespoons) Irish
   wholegrain mustard
6 fl oz (175 ml/¾ cup)
   light cream

Garnish
chopped fresh parsley

Serves 4 as a starter

Remove the skin, membrane and 'plumbing' from the kidneys. Cut into bite-sized pieces. Sauté in a little butter in a pan on a medium heat, turning occasionally until nicely cooked — 5 minutes approx. Season with salt and freshly ground pepper. Add the mustard and cream, bring to the boil and simmer 3-4 minutes until the sauce thickens slightly. Taste and correct the seasoning. Serve immediately, sprinkled with parsley.

BEEF

Steak with Mushroom à la Crème and Thyme Leaves
Elizabeth's Mustard Burgers
Stir-fried Beef with Crispy Vegetables and Oyster Sauce
* Mexican Mince with Tacos and Tomato Salsa
Spicy Indian Mince with Fluffy Rice
Chilli con Carne

Steak with Mushroom à la Crème and Thyme Leaves

6 × 6 oz (170 g) sirloin
   or fillet steaks

1 clove of garlic
salt and freshly ground pepper

a little extra virgin olive oil
1 quantity **Mushroom à la Crème**
recipe (see page 102)
1 teaspoon thyme leaves

Garnish
fresh watercress *or* parsley

Serves 6

Cut a clove of garlic in half, rub both sides of each steak with the cut clove, grind some black pepper over the steaks and sprinkle on a few drops of olive oil. Turn the steaks in the oil and leave aside while you heat the grill pan. If using sirloin steaks, score the fat at 1 inch (2.5 cm) intervals.

Season the steaks with a little salt and put them on to the hot grill pan. Meanwhile heat the Mushroom à la Crème, add thyme leaves and correct the seasoning.

The approximate cooking times for each side of the steaks are:

	SIRLOIN	FILLET
rare	2 minutes	5 minutes
medium-rare	3 minutes	6 minutes
medium	4 minutes	7 minutes
well done	5 minutes	8-9 minutes

If serving sirloin steak, at the end of the cooking time turn it over on to the fat with a tongs and cook for 2-3 minutes until the fat becomes crisp.

To serve, put the steaks on to hot plates. Spoon the warm Mushroom à la Crème over one end of each and garnish with fresh watercress or parsley sprigs.

Elizabeth's Mustard Burgers

I am indebted to my sister Elizabeth for this delicious recipe.

1 lb (450 g) freshly minced beef
¼ oz (8 g/½ American
tablespoon) butter
2 oz (55 g/scant ½ cup) onion,
finely chopped
1 teaspoon finely chopped parsley
1 teaspoon thyme leaves
1½ tablespoons (2 American
tablespoons) Ballymaloe
Country Relish

2 teaspoons English mustard
salt and freshly
ground pepper
seasoned flour
olive oil
Mushroom à la Crème
(see page 102)

Garnish
rocket leaves (optional)

Serves 4

Melt the butter in a heavy-bottomed saucepan, sweat the onion until soft but not coloured and allow to cool. Mix the minced beef with the chopped parsley and thyme leaves. Add the Ballymaloe Country Relish, mustard and sweated onion. Season with salt and freshly ground pepper and mix well. Fry a little morsel to taste the seasoning.

Shape the mixture into 4 hamburgers with wet hands; toss in seasoned flour, and cook in a little olive oil in a hot pan. Serve immediately, smothered in Mushroom à la Crème. Garnish with rocket leaves if available.

Stir-fried Beef with Crispy Vegetables and Oyster Sauce

B*ottles of oyster sauce can be found in virtually any supermarket nowadays. Once opened it will last for several months — longer if you keep it in the fridge. Despite the name it doesn't taste of oysters but is a delicious flavour enhancer.*

12-14 oz (350–400 g) beef steak — e.g. rump
1 teaspoon sugar
1 tablespoon approx. light soy sauce
2 tablespoons approx. rice wine *or* dry sherry
2 teaspoons cornflour, slaked with 1 tablespoon water
4 oz (110 g) bamboo shoots *or* celery, sliced thinly at an angle
4 oz (110 g/scant 1 cup) thinly sliced carrots
4 oz (110 g) broccoli
4 oz (110 g) courgettes *or* mangetout peas *or* a mixture
4 tablespoons (5½ American tablespoons) sunflower *or* peanut oil
2 tablespoons (2½ American tablespoons) spring onion, sliced at an angle into ¼ inch (5 mm) pieces
½ teaspoon peeled and grated fresh root ginger
1 scant teaspoon salt
1 teaspoon sugar
a little stock *or* water
2-3 tablespoons (2½-4 American tablespoons) oyster sauce

Serves 6-8

Cut the beef into thin slices about the size of a large postage stamp. Marinate in the sugar, soy sauce, wine and cornflour for 25-30 minutes while you prepare the vegetables.

Cut the bamboo shoots and carrots into roughly the same size as the beef. Slice the broccoli or courgettes into small pieces also, if using, or top and tail the mangetout peas.

Heat the oil in a preheated wok,

stir-fry the beef for 30-40 seconds approx. or until the colour changes, then quickly remove with a slotted spoon. Into the same oil, add the spring onion, ginger and the vegetables. Stir-fry for 2-3 minutes, then add the salt, sugar and a little stock or water if necessary. Now add the beef and oyster sauce and blend. Stir for one more minute and serve hot.

* Mexican Mince with Tacos and Tomato Salsa

*M*ince cooked in this Mexican way is absolutely addictive — I adore all the accompaniments! Keep a few packets of tacos in your store-cupboard to nibble with Mexican Mince and Chilli con Carne.

1 lb (450 g) freshly minced beef
2 tablespoons approx.
    sunflower oil
6 oz (170 g/generous 1 cup)
    onion, chopped
2 cloves of garlic, crushed
1 teaspoon freshly ground cumin
2 teaspoons chopped annual
    marjoram *or* oregano
1 fresh chilli, deseeded and
    chopped *or* a pinch of
    chilli powder *or* 1 teaspoon
    chilli sauce
a good dash of soy sauce
salt, freshly ground black pepper
    and a pinch of sugar

Accompaniments
Tomato and Coriander Salsa
    (see below)
Guacamole (see page 14)
shredded crispy lettuce
sour cream
grated Cheddar cheese
tacos

Serves 6

Heat the oil in a frying pan, add the chopped onion and garlic and cook over a medium heat until soft and slightly golden. Increase the heat, add the minced beef and stir until brown. Add the cumin, marjoram or oregano and chilli. Then shake in the soy sauce and season well with salt, freshly ground pepper and sugar. Taste, because this mixture needs a surprising amount of salt.

Serve with Tomato and Coriander Salsa, Guacamole, shredded crispy lettuce, sour cream, grated Cheddar cheese and Tacos. Put them together in whatever combination you fancy and enjoy!

TOMATO AND CORIANDER SALSA
This sauce is ever-present on Mexican tables.

2 very ripe tomatoes, chopped
1 tablespoon approx.
    chopped onion
1 clove of garlic, crushed
½-1 chilli, deseeded and
    finely chopped

1-2 tablespoons approx. chopped
    fresh coriander
a squeeze of fresh lime juice
salt, freshly ground pepper
    and sugar

Mix all the ingredients together.
Season with salt, freshly ground
pepper and sugar.

Spicy Indian Mince with Fluffy Rice

*N*ot surprisingly when fresh spices are
added, boring old mince is infused
with the magical flavours of India —
Madhur Jaffrey inspires again.

2 lb (900 g) freshly minced lamb
    or beef
2 bay leaves
1 cinnamon stick, 3 inches
    (7.5 cm) long
6 whole cloves
2 tablespoons approx. sunflower
    or peanut oil
6 oz (170 g/generous 1 cup)
    approx. onion, finely chopped
a piece of fresh root ginger, 1
    inch (2.5 cm) square, finely
    chopped *or* grated
4 cloves of garlic, crushed
1 tablespoon (1 generous
    American tablespoon) freshly
    ground coriander
1 tablespoon (1 generous
    American tablespoon) freshly
    ground cumin
1 tablespoon (1 generous
    American tablespoon) ground
    turmeric
2 tablespoons (2½ American
    tablespoons) plain yoghurt

1 medium sized tomato, peeled
    and chopped *or* tinned
    equivalent
¼ teaspoon ground mace
¼ teaspoon ground nutmeg
1 teaspoon salt
a good pinch of cayenne pepper
    (optional)
4 fl oz (120 ml/½ cup) water

Accompaniments
Fluffy Rice (see below)
Crispy Onion Rings (see below)

Serves 6

Put the bay leaves, cinnamon and
cloves in the hot oil. After a few
seconds when the bay leaves begin to
darken and the cinnamon starts to
uncurl, add the onion, ginger and
garlic. Fry for 6–8 minutes until the
onion starts to caramelise at the edges.
Reduce the heat and add the
coriander, cumin and turmeric. Fry
for 2 minutes approx., stirring all the
time. Add the yoghurt and cook,
stirring for another minute. Then put
in the chopped tomato and continue
to fry and stir for 2–3 minutes.

Add the mince. Raise the heat and fry and stir for 7–8 minutes. Then put in the mace, nutmeg, salt, cayenne pepper (if using) and water. Stir, bring to the boil, cover, turn heat down to low and allow to simmer while you cook the rice (see below).

Just before serving, remove the cinnamon stick. Serve with Fluffy Rice (see below) and perhaps Crispy Onion Rings (see below) so beloved in India and indeed the world over.

FLUFFY RICE

T his is my favourite recipe for foolproof rice.

12 oz (340 g/1½ cups) long grain rice — e.g. Basmati
4 pints (2.3 L/10 cups) water
2 teaspoons salt
½–1 oz (15–30 g/⅛–¼ stick) butter
chopped fresh herbs (optional)

Serves 4

Bring the water to the boil, add the salt and sprinkle the rice into the fast-boiling water, stirring as you do so.

Boil for 7 minutes approx. or until the grains have almost doubled in length but still have a very slight bite when tested. Drain and turn into a hot serving dish. Cover with tinfoil and allow to sit in a warm place while you put the rest of the meal on the table.

Taste the rice, correct the seasoning if necessary and fork in the butter and some herbs if you fancy.

CRISPY ONION RINGS
1 medium-sized onion, cut into very thin slices
4 tablespoons (5 generous American tablespoons) sunflower *or* peanut oil

Heat the oil in a heavy-bottomed 10-12 inch (25–30 cm) frying-pan, over a medium heat. Fry the onion rings in hot oil for 5 minutes approx. or until dark brown but not burnt; drain well. Remove with a slotted spoon and spread on paper towels.

Chilli con Carne

P rovided I'm not in a frantic rush, I prefer to use cubed stewing beef for Chilli Con Carne. However, mince cooks faster.

1–1½ lb (450–675 g) freshly minced beef
1–2 tablespoons extra virgin olive oil
1 large onion, chopped

2-3 cloves of garlic, crushed
1 small green pepper, deseeded
    and sliced
1 quantity Chilli Pepper Sauce
    (see below) *or* 1-2 teaspoons
    chilli powder
1 tablespoon (1 generous
    American tablespoon)
    tomato concentrate
1 teaspoon ground cumin
4-8 oz (110-225 g) red kidney
    beans, cooked *or* tinned
salt,
a little brown sugar

Accompaniments
Fluffy Rice (see above)
Tacos (optional)
Guacamole (optional — see
    page 14)
sour cream
mature Cheddar cheese

Garnish
fresh coriander leaves

Serves 4-6

Heat the oil in a pan, brown the
onion and garlic lightly, add the
pepper and cook for a few minutes
while you make the chilli sauce.
Add the mince and toss until it looses
its raw colour. Add the Chilli Pepper
Sauce and just enough water to
cover the ingredients. Cover the
saucepan tightly and leave to stew
until cooked, 10 minutes approx.,
keeping the heat low. Check the
liquid level occasionally. By the end
of the cooking time it should have
reduced to a brownish red and
rather thick sauce.

Finally add the tomato
concentrate, the cumin and the
cooked kidney beans. Season with
salt and brown sugar to taste. Simmer
for a further 15 minutes, correct the
seasoning and serve with rice, Tacos,
Guacamole, sour cream and grated
Cheddar cheese. Garnish with lots
of fresh coriander leaves.

CHILLI PEPPER SAUCE

*T*his *delicious sauce gives a much
better flavour than bought chilli
powder. We also use it as a marinading
mixture and of course as a sauce to perk
up other dishes.*

4-5 large fresh chillies
1 large red pepper, chopped
1 large onion, chopped
1 large clove of garlic
salt to taste

Cut the stalks off the chillies and
discard the seeds. Purée the flesh with
the other ingredients, using a
tablespoon or two of water if
necessary. Salt is very important in
this recipe to enhance the flavour.
This sauce may be frozen or kept in
a covered container in the fridge for
2-3 days.

PORK

Pork or Chicken with Mushrooms
Pork or Chicken with Mushrooms
and Fresh Ginger
* Homemade Sausages with Bramley Apple Sauce
and Scallion Champ
Homemade Sausages with Coriander
* Thai Stir-fried Pork with Ginger and Coriander

Pork or Chicken with Mushrooms

You can use the formula of this quick and delicious recipe for fillet steak instead of pork or chicken breast, but be careful not to overcook the meat. If you haven't got any wine to hand just add a little more stock.

2 lb (900 g) pork fillet *or* chicken
breast — naturally reared
if possible
1-2 tablespoons extra virgin
olive *or* sunflower oil
or a little butter
4 oz (110 g/scant 1 cup) onion,
finely chopped
¼ pint (150 ml/generous ½ cup)
homemade chicken stock
8 oz (225 g/4 cups)
mushrooms, sliced
½ pint (300 ml/1¼ cups)
light cream
a little roux (see glossary)
2 tablespoons approx. chopped
fresh parsley
freshly squeezed lemon juice
salt and freshly ground pepper

Accompaniments
Orzo (see page 60) *or* **Fluffy Rice
(see page 31)**

Serves 6-8

Cut the pork or chicken into slices ⅓ inch (8 mm) thick approx. Pour a little of the oil or butter into a very hot frying pan and sauté the pieces of meat, a few at a time, until brown on both sides but not fully cooked. Remove to a plate and keep warm.

Add a little more oil or butter and cook the onion gently until soft and golden. Deglaze the pan, add the stock and boil to reduce by one-quarter. Meanwhile sauté the mushrooms in a little oil or butter in another frying pan over a high heat, then add to the pork or chicken.

Add the cream to the onion and stock, then bring back to the boil, thicken slightly with roux, add the meat, mushrooms and parsley to the sauce and all the juices. Taste, add a

little lemon juice and bubble gently
for a couple of minutes until the meat
is fully cooked. Taste again and
correct the seasoning if necessary.

Pour into a hot serving dish
and serve with Orzo or a bowl of
fluffy rice.

PORK OR CHICKEN WITH MUSHROOMS AND FRESH GINGER

Add 1-2 tablespoons of freshly
grated root ginger to the onion
while it is sweating. Continue as in
the master recipe.

*Homemade Sausages with Bramley Apple Sauce and Scallion Champ

*Homemade sausages are just as easy to
prepare as hamburgers and make a
cheap and comforting meal.*

1 lb (450 g) fat streaky pork
2-4 teaspoons mixed fresh herbs
— parsley, thyme, chives,
marjoram and rosemary
***or* sage**
2½ oz (70 g/generous 1 cup)
soft white breadcrumbs
1 egg — free-range if possible
1 large clove of garlic, crushed
salt and freshly ground pepper
a little oil

Bramley Apple Sauce (see below)
Scallion Champ (see page 105)

Serves 6-8 — makes 12-16 approx.

Mince the pork. Chop the herbs
finely and mix through the crumbs.
Crush the garlic to a paste with a little
salt. Whisk the egg, then mix all the
ingredients together thoroughly,
including the seasoning.

Fry off a little knob of the
mixture to check the seasoning, and
correct it if necessary. Divide into 16
pieces and roll into lengths. Fry gently
on a barely oiled pan until golden on
all sides.

These sausages are particularly
delicious served with Bramley Apple
Sauce and a big bowl of buttery
Scallion Champ.

BRAMLEY APPLE SAUCE

*The trick with apple sauce is to cook it
on a very low heat with only a tiny
drop of water so that it is nice and thick.*

*It is always worth having some in the
freezer in little tubs in case you feel like a
juicy pork chop for supper.*

1 lb (450 g) cooking apples —
Bramley Seedling *or* Grenadier
if possible
1-2 dessertspoons (1½-2½
American teaspoons) water
2 oz (55 g/¼ cup) approx. sugar
(depending on how tart the
apples are)

Peel, quarter and core the apples; cut the pieces in two and put them in a stainless or cast-iron saucepan, with the water and sugar. Cover and cook on a very low heat until the apples break down in a fluff. Stir and taste for sweetness.

Serve warm or cold.

HOMEMADE SAUSAGES WITH CORIANDER

F *or a change I recently substituted 2 tablespoons of fresh coriander for the mixed herbs in the sausage mixture and found it completely delicious. I also added a good pinch of sugar to enhance the sweetness in the oriental way. If you want to continue in that vein serve the sausages with Thai Dipping Sauce (see page 38) instead of the more traditional Scallion Champ (see page 105) and Bramley Apple Sauce (above).*

* Thai Stir-fried Pork with Ginger and Coriander

T *he quantity of fresh ginger may seem extraordinary here, but it tastes great — so don't be tempted to reduce it.*

1 lb (450 g) pork fillet
2 teaspoons cornflour
2 tablespoons (2 generous
American tablespoons)
sesame oil
a good pinch of salt
3 tablespoons (4 American
tablespoons) sunflower *or*
arachide oil
4 tablespoons (5 generous
American tablespoons) finely
chopped fresh root ginger
2 tablespoons (2 generous

American tablespoons) nam
pla (fish sauce)
2 tablespoons (2 generous
American tablespoons)
soy sauce
1 teaspoon sugar
freshly ground pepper

Garnish
fresh coriander leaves

Serves 4-6

Trim the pork fillet and cut into ¼ inch (5 mm) thick slices. Cut each slice into quarters. Put into a bowl and toss well with the cornflour, sesame oil and salt. Leave to marinate for 20-30 minutes.

Just before eating, heat the sunflower or arachide oil in a wok, add the ginger and stir-fry until just beginning to crisp (this may take 2-3 minutes but it is worth persevering).

Add the pork and toss until it changes colour, then add the fish sauce, soy sauce, sugar and lots of freshly ground pepper. Taste and correct the seasoning if necessary.

Turn into a hot serving dish and garnish with fresh coriander leaves.

Fish

* *Goujons of Plaice, Sole or Monkfish*
with Various Sauces
* *Crispy Fish with Tartare Sauce*
* *Fish and Chips*
Salmon with Tomato and Basil
Salmon with Tomato and Fresh Parsley
Trout with Cream and Dill
Pangrilled Fish with Flavoured Butters
or Avocado Salsa
* **Mackerel Sandwich with Mushrooms and Fresh Herbs**
Fish in Paper Parcels with Hollandaise Sauce
Papillote of Salmon with Tomato Concassé and Basil
Papillote of Salmon with Ginger Butter
Papillote of Salmon with Cucumber and Dill or Fennel
Papillote of Salmon with Fresh Herbs
Baked Cod Niçoise

I've said many times before that fish is the ultimate fast food. So convinced am I of this that I have already written an entire book on the subject: *Simply Delicious Fish*. There you will find many delectable recipes which are absolutely unbeatable for speed — for example, Warm Smoked Salmon with cucumber and dill, and Trout with ginger butter.

Provided that fish is really fresh,

the simpler the cooking method, the better. It's hard to improve on a piece of perfectly fresh pangrilled fish with a simple herb butter. For some reason which is absolutely beyond my comprehension, very few restaurants seem to be able to resist the temptation to pile on all sorts of fancy, and usually unnecessary, embellishments.

* Goujons of Plaice, Sole or Monkfish with Various Sauces

Whatever the coating, this is a great recipe to make a little fish go a long way.

6-8 skinned fillets of sole
or plaice or 1-2 medium-sized
monkfish tails

extra virgin olive oil *or*
    sunflower oil for deep-frying

Batter
5 oz (140 g/1 cup) plain
    white flour
2 tablespoons (2 generous
    American tablespoons)
    extra virgin olive oil
water
1-1½ egg whites
sea salt

Garnish
segments of lemon
sprigs of parsley

Suggested accompaniments
Thai Dipping Sauce
    (see below)
Homemade Mayonnaise
    (see opposite)
Garlic Mayonnaise
    (see page 40)
Orly Sauce
    (see page 40)
Quick Tartare Sauce
    (see page 40)

Serves 6-8 as a main course

First make the batter base. Sieve the
flour into a bowl, make a well in the
centre, pour in the olive oil, stir and
add enough water to make a batter
about the consistency of double
cream. Allow to stand.

Cut the fish into ½ inch (1 cm)
strips on the bias. Heat the oil in
the deep-frier to very hot —
200°C/400°F. Just before serving,
whisk the egg whites to a stiff peak
and fold into the batter, adding a
good pinch of sea salt. Dip each
goujon individually into the batter
and drop into the hot oil. Fry until
golden (1-2 minutes approx.) and
drain on kitchen paper.

Serve at once on hot plates with
a tiny bowl, shell or edible container
full of the sauce of your choice in
the centre. Garnish each plate with
a segment of lemon and a sprig
of parsley.

We sometimes hollow out tiny
tomatoes or chunks of cucumber, to
hold the sauce. Courgette blossoms
also make delightful edible containers.

THAI DIPPING SAUCE

A version of this sauce is ever present on
restaurant tables in Thailand and
Vietnam. It is a great dipping sauce to use
with grilled or deep-fried meat or fish —
and of course spring rolls.

3 tablespoons (4 American
    tablespoons) nam pla
    (fish sauce)
3 tablespoons (4 American
    tablespoons) freshly squeezed
    lime *or* lemon juice

2 tablespoons approx. sugar
 or more to taste
3 tablespoons water
1 clove of garlic, crushed
3-4 fresh hot red
 or green chillies

Serves 4

Combine the fish sauce, freshly squeezed juice, sugar and water in a jar, and add the garlic. Mix well and pour into four individual bowls. Cut the chillies crosswise into very thin rounds and divide them between the bowls.

HOMEMADE MAYONNAISE

I know it is very tempting to reach for a jar of 'well known brand', but most people don't seem to be aware that mayonnaise can be made, even with a hand whisk, in under 5 minutes. If you use a food processor the technique is still the same but the time is just a couple of minutes. The great secret is to have all your ingredients at room temperature and to drip the oil very slowly into the egg yolks at the beginning. The quality of the mayonnaise will depend totally on the quality of the egg yolks, oil and vinegar you use.

2 egg yolks, free-range
 if possible
¼ teaspoon salt
a pinch of English mustard
 or ¼ teaspoon French mustard
15 ml/1 dessertspoon white
 wine vinegar
8 fl oz (250 ml/1 cup) oil
 (sunflower, arachide
 or extra virgin olive oil,
 or a mixture — we use
 6 fl oz (175 ml) arachide oil
 and 2 fl oz (50 ml) extra
 virgin olive oil

Put the egg yolks into a bowl with the salt, mustard and white wine vinegar. (Keep the whites to make meringues.) Put the oil into a measure. Take a whisk in one hand and the oil in the other and drip the oil slowly on to the egg yolks, whisking all the time. Within a minute you will notice that the mixture is beginning to thicken. When this happens you can add the oil a little faster, but don't get too cheeky or it will suddenly curdle because the egg yolks can only absorb the oil at a certain pace. Taste and add a little more seasoning and vinegar if necessary.

If the mayonnaise curdles it will suddenly become quite thin, and if left sitting the oil will start to float to the top of the sauce. If this happens you can rectify the situation. Put another egg yolk or 1-2 tablespoons of boiling water into a clean bowl, then whisk in the curdled mayonnaise, half a teaspoonful at a time until it emulsifies again.

Serve with cold cooked meats, fowl, fish, eggs and vegetables.

GARLIC MAYONNAISE
ingredients as above
1-4 cloves of garlic, depending on size
2 teaspoons chopped fresh parsley

Crush the garlic and add to the egg yolks just as you start to make the mayonnaise. Add the parsley at the end and taste for seasoning.

Note: Here is a tip for crushing garlic. Put the whole clove of garlic on a board, preferably one that is reserved for garlic and onions. Tap the clove with a flat blade of a chopping knife, to break the skin. Remove the skin and discard. Then sprinkle a few grains of salt on to the clove. Again using the flat blade of the knife, keep pressing the tip of the knife down on to the garlic to form a paste. The salt provides friction and ensures the clove won't shoot off the board!

ORLY SAUCE

8 tablespoons (10 American tablespoons) Homemade Mayonnaise (see above)
1-2 teaspoons concentrated tomato purée
salt, freshly ground pepper and sugar

Mix the tomato purée with the mayonnaise, season with salt and freshly ground pepper and sugar. Taste and correct the seasoning if necessary.

QUICK TARTARE SAUCE

The classic Tartare Sauce takes rather longer to make but this also tastes great, provided the base mayonnaise is good.

½ pint (300 ml/1¼ cups) mayonnaise, homemade if possible (see page 39)
1 large hardboiled egg
1 teaspoon chopped capers
1 teaspoon chopped gherkin
2 teaspoons chopped chives
**   *or* spring onion**
2 teaspoons chopped fresh parsley
salt and freshly ground pepper to taste

Serves 8 approx.

Separate the yolk from the white of the hardboiled egg. Sieve the yolk into the bowl of mayonnaise. Stir and then add in the other ingredients — capers, gherkin, chives or spring onion and parsley. Roughly chop the hardboiled egg white and fold in gently. Taste and season if necessary with salt and freshly ground pepper.

*Crispy Fish with Tartare Sauce

V irtually any fish can be cooked
    this way but be careful that the fillet
is not too thick or it may be overcooked
on the outside but still underdone in
the centre. A Gigas oyster shell makes
a pretty container for the sauce on
each plate.

4 fresh mackerel, plaice
    or lemon sole
white flour seasoned
    with salt and freshly
    ground pepper
2 eggs, whisked with
    a little milk
fresh white breadcrumbs
extra virgin olive or sunflower
    oil for deep-frying

Garnish
lemon segments
sprigs of parsley

Accompaniment
Tartare Sauce (see opposite)

Serves 4 as a main course, 8 as a starter

Gut and wash the fish. Fillet carefully
and dry on kitchen paper. Preheat the
deep-frier to 180°C/350°F. Coat
each piece of fish first in seasoned
flour, then in beaten egg and finally
in crumbs. When the oil is hot
enough, fry a few fillets at a time.
Drain on kitchen paper.

Serve on hot plates with a
segment of lemon, a sprig of fresh
parsley and Tartare Sauce.

*Fish and Chips

F ish and chips became famous because
    they can be utterly delicious. The fish
needs to be spanking fresh, the batter crisp,
the potatoes a good variety and most
importantly of all, the oil needs to be of
good quality. In Spain and Greece olive
oil is frequently used, but sunflower or
arachide can be excellent also. Don't
bother to peel the potatoes. They taste
much more delicious with the skin on, and
are also better for you.

8 very fresh fillets of cod,
    haddock, plaice,
    or lemon sole

Batter
5 oz (140 g/1 cup) plain flour
2 tablespoons (2 generous
    American tablespoons)
    extra virgin olive oil
water
1-1½ egg whites
sea salt

Chips
8-16 well scrubbed
    unpeeled potatoes

Garnish
1 lemon

Accompaniment
vinegar
Tartare Sauce (see page 40)
   or **Orly Sauce (see page 40)**

Serves 8

First make the batter (see page 38).

Cut the potatoes into chips of whatever size you fancy (remember the bigger they are, the longer they take to cook). Heat the oil in the deep-frier and add the chips. Make sure they are absolutely dry and don't cook too many together.) Cook for a few minutes until they are pale golden and just soft, then drain.

Dip the fish fillets in batter, allow the excess to drip off and lower gently into the oil, shaking the basket at the same time. Cook until crisp and golden and drain on kitchen paper.

Increase the heat to 190°C/375°F. Put the chips back in to the oil and cook for a minute or two until really crisp and golden. Drain on kitchen paper and sprinkle with salt.

Serve the fish and chips immediately, either on a plate or in a cornet of paper, garnished with a lemon wedge. Serve vinegar as an accompaniment. Tartare Sauce or Orly Sauce makes a delicious accompanying dip.

Teeny Weeny Fish and Chips

I*t's fun to serve scaled down fish and chips as canapés with drinks.*

Put freshly cooked goujons of plaice, sole or monkfish and freshly cooked fine chips in tiny cornets of plain paper and serve very hot.

Salmon with Tomato and Basil

F*armed salmon is now widely available all year round, but be sure to use wild Irish salmon in season.*

4 × 2 oz (55 g) escalopes of
   salmon, skinned
salt and freshly ground pepper

1 oz (30 g/¼ stick) butter
2 tablespoons approx. finely
   chopped spring onion
4 tablespoons
   (5 American tablespoons)
   tomato concassé
   (see glossary)

2 teaspoons freshly torn basil
a pinch of sugar

non-stick frying pan

Serves 4 as a starter

First prepare all the ingredients.

Just before serving, heat the non-stick frying pan. Season the salmon with salt and freshly ground pepper, and cook for just a few seconds on each side on the dry pan. Remove to four hot plates. Melt the butter, add the spring onion and cook for a few seconds. Add the tomato concassé and basil. Season with salt, freshly ground pepper and a pinch of sugar and cook for a few seconds. The tomato should just warm through but should not be cooked. Taste, spoon over the fish and serve immediately.

SALMON WITH TOMATO AND FRESH PARSLEY

S ubstitute 3 teaspoons of chopped fresh parsley for basil in the above recipe.

Trout with Cream and Dill

L ittle rainbow trout are available in virtually every fish shop. This combination is surprisingly delicious and very fast to cook. If dill is difficult to find, use a mixture of fresh herbs.

4 fresh trout
salt and freshly ground pepper
¼ oz (8 g/½ American
**   tablespoon) butter**
6 fl oz (175 ml/¾ cup) cream
1½-2 tablespoons approx. finely
**   chopped fresh dill**

Serves 4

Gut the trout, fillet carefully, wash and dry well. Season with salt and freshly ground pepper. Melt the butter in a frying pan and fry the trout fillets flesh side down until golden brown. Turn over on to the skin side, add the cream and dill. Simmer gently for 3-4 minutes or until the trout is cooked. Taste the sauce to check the seasoning and serve immediately.

Pangrilled Fish with Flavoured Butters or Avocado Salsa

*P*angrilling is one of my favourite ways to cook fish, meat and vegetables. Square or oblong cast-iron pangrills can be bought in virtually all good kitchen shops and are a 'must have' as far as I am concerned. In this recipe you can use almost any fish — mackerel, grey sea mullet, cod, sea bass, haddock — provided it is very fresh.

**8 × 6 oz (170 g) of very
  fresh fish fillets**
seasoned flour
a small knob of butter

Garnish
sprigs of parsley
segment of lemon

Accompaniment
**Flavoured Butter (see below) *or*
  Tomato Fondue (see page
  101) *or* Avocado Salsa
  (see page 46)**

Serves 4 as a main course (use 3 oz fillets for a starter)

Heat the pangrill. Dip the fish fillets in flour which has been well seasoned with salt and freshly ground pepper. Shake off the excess and spread a little butter with a knife on the flesh side as though you were buttering a slice of bread rather meanly. When the pangrill is quite hot but not smoking, place the fish fillets butter side down on the grill; the fish should sizzle as soon as it touches the pan. Turn down the heat slightly and cook for 4-5 minutes on that side (time depends on the thickness of the fish).

Turn over and cook on the other side until crisp and golden. Serve on a hot plate with a segment of lemon and some slices of the flavoured butter of your choice or the Salsa. The flavoured butter may be served directly on top of the fish, or if you have a pretty shell, place it at the side of the plate as a butter container. Garnish with parsley and a segment of lemon.

Note: Fish under 2 lb (900 g) such as mackerel, herring and brown trout can also be grilled whole on the pan. Large fish (4-6 lb/2-3 kg) may also be grilled whole. Cook for 10-15 minutes approx. on each side and then put in a hot oven for another 15 minutes approx. to finish cooking.

The following are good things to serve with pangrilled fish.

PARSLEY OR FRESH HERB BUTTER

4 oz (110 g/1 stick) butter
finely chopped fresh parsley *or* a
   mixture of chopped fresh
   herbs — parsley, chives,
   thyme, fennel, lemon balm
a few drops of freshly squeezed
   lemon juice

Cream the butter and add in the parsley or mixed herbs and a few drops of lemon juice. Roll into butter pats or form into a roll and wrap in greaseproof paper or tinfoil, screwing each end so that it looks like a cracker. Refrigerate to harden.

GRAINY MUSTARD BUTTER

T his is particularly good with mackerel or herring.

4 oz (110 g/1 stick) butter
1 tablespoon (1 generous
   American tablespoon)
   Dijon mustard

2 teaspoons (1 generous American
   tablespoon) grainy mustard

Cream the butter, add both mustards, put into a bowl and cover or form into a roll and refrigerate until needed.

OLIVE AND ANCHOVY BUTTER

4 oz (110 g/1 stick) butter
1-2 anchovies
4 black olives, stoned
2 teaspoons approx. chopped
   fresh parsley

Whizz all the ingredients together in a food processor or chop the ingredients finely and mix with the butter. Put in a bowl and cover or form into a roll and refrigerate until needed.

CHILLI AND CORIANDER BUTTER

4 oz (110 g/1 stick) butter
1 chilli, finely chopped
1 tablespoon approx. chopped
   fresh coriander *or* marjoram
freshly ground pepper
a few drops of lime *or* lemon juice

Cream the butter, then add the chilli and fresh herbs. Season with freshly ground pepper and lime or lemon juice. Put in a bowl and cover or form into a roll and refrigerate until needed.

AVOCADO SALSA

Now that Tomato Salsa is becoming more familiar, you may feel like a change from the classic Mexican version.

1 avocado
2 ripe tomatoes
1 tablespoon approx. finely
    chopped spring onion
1 clove of garlic, crushed
1 chilli, deseeded and
    finely chopped
¼–½ teaspoon lightly roasted
    cumin seeds, crushed

1–2 tablespoons approx. roughly
    chopped fresh coriander
salt and freshly ground pepper

Serves 4 approx.

Cut the avocado flesh and the tomatoes into ¼ inch (5 mm) dice, and add the spring onion and chilli. Mix with the other ingredients in a bowl. Taste.

*Mackerel Sandwich with Mushrooms and Fresh Herbs

This delicious 'sandwich' transforms the humble mackerel into something quite trendy and utterly delicious.

4 very fresh mackerel
seasoned flour
½ oz (15 g/⅛ stick) butter
4 oz (110 g) mushrooms,
    finely chopped
4 teaspoons finely chopped fresh
    herbs — thyme, parsley,
    chives, fennel, lemon balm
1–2 cloves of garlic, crushed

Garnish
fresh herbs
chive flowers if available

Serves 4

Fillet the mackerel, wash, dry and dip in flour which has been well seasoned with salt and freshly ground pepper. Spread a little soft butter evenly over the flesh side of each fillet. Heat a frying pan or cast-iron pangrill large enough to take the fish in a single layer. Sauté until golden on both sides.

Remove the fish to a hot serving dish or four individual plates. Add the mushrooms and garlic to the pan. Cook for 2-3 minutes, add the fresh herbs and season with a little salt and freshly ground pepper if necessary. Divide the mixture in four. Spoon a quarter over four of the fillets and top each with another fillet, crispy side upwards. Garnish with a sprig of fresh herbs and perhaps a few chive flowers. Serve immediately.

Note: This mushroom, garlic and herb mixture is also delicious served with sautéed chicken livers on toast, as a first course.

Lamb Chops with Aubergine and Tomato Fondue

Homemade Sausages with Bramley Apple Sauce and Scallion Champ

Fish and Chips

Preparation of Penne with Red and Yellow Peppers and Basil Leaves

Pasta Salad with Tuna and Beans

Macaroni Cheese

Fish in Paper Parcels with Hollandaise Sauce

G rey sea mullet, sea bass, monkfish, trout or salmon are all quite delicious served in this way. Each person should have the special delight of opening their own papillote with its tantalising aroma. A little Hollandaise Sauce, which can be made while the fish is cooking makes this into a feast. Alternatively, you may vary the contents of the little parcel along the lines suggested in the recipes included here for salmon.

Per person
**4 oz (110 g) piece of fresh
    fish, skinned
sea salt and freshly
    ground pepper
a little butter
sprig of fresh fennel *or* dill**

Accompaniment
Hollandaise Sauce (see below)

greaseproof paper

Salt the fish on both sides and leave for 10 minutes if possible. Preheat the oven to 180°C/350°F/regulo 4. Fold the greaseproof paper in half, smear a little butter on the underneath piece and place the fish on it. Season with freshly ground pepper, and put a little more butter and a sprig of fennel or dill on top.

Fold the paper over and seal the edges well. Bake in a preheated moderate oven for 10–12 minutes. Serve immediately with a little Hollandaise Sauce.

HOLLANDAISE SAUCE

T his exquisite sauce which can transform even the simplest piece of fish into a feast can be made well within 5 minutes.

**2 egg yolks, free-range
if possible
1 dessertspoon (2 teaspoons)
    cold water
4 oz (110 g/1 stick) butter, diced
1 teaspoon approx. lemon juice
salt and freshly ground pepper**

Serves 6-8

Put the egg yolks into a heavy-bottomed stainless steel saucepan on a very low heat, or in a bowl over hot water. Add the water and whisk thoroughly. Add the butter bit by bit, whisking all the time. As soon as one piece melts, add the next piece.

The mixture will gradually thicken, but if it shows signs of becoming too thick or slightly 'scrambling', remove from the heat immediately and add a little cold water if necessary. Do not leave the pan or stop whisking until the sauce is made.

Finally add the lemon juice and salt and pepper to taste. Pour into a bowl and keep warm over hot but not boiling water.

If the sauce is slow to thicken it may be because you are excessively cautious and the heat is too low. Increase the heat slightly and continue to whisk until the sauce thickens to light coating consistency.

Fish in Paper Parcels – Variations

PAPILLOTE OF SALMON WITH TOMATO CONCASSÉ AND BASIL

Per person
**4 oz (110 g) piece of
   fresh salmon
1 tablespoon tomato concassé
   (see glossary)
salt, freshly ground pepper
   and sugar
2 leaves fresh basil
½ oz (15 g/⅛ stick) butter**

Season the tomato concassé well with salt, freshly ground pepper and sugar. Put the salmon on the lightly buttered greaseproof paper, with 1 basil leaf underneath and one on top. Spoon the tomato concassé over and add a good knob of butter. Seal the package and proceed as before.

PAPILLOTE OF SALMON WITH GINGER BUTTER

Per person
**4 oz (110 g) piece of fresh salmon
salt**

Ginger Butter
**2 oz (55 g/½ stick) butter
3 teaspoons finely grated fresh
   ginger root
1 teaspoon finely chopped
   fresh parsley**

First make the ginger butter by beating the ginger and parsley into the butter. Salt the salmon on both sides and leave for 10 minutes if possible. Proceed as in the master recipe, using a blob of ginger butter with each piece of fish.

PAPILLOTE OF SALMON WITH CUCUMBER AND DILL OR FENNEL

Per person
**4 oz (110 g) piece of
   fresh salmon
salt
1 tablespoon approx. finely
   diced cucumber**

**a little butter
a good pinch of chopped
   fresh dill *or* ½ teaspoon
   chopped fresh fennel
salt and freshly
   ground pepper**

Salt the salmon on both sides and leave for 10 minutes if possible. Sweat the cucumber briefly in the butter. Proceed as in the master recipe (page 47) putting the cucumber and herbs on top of the fish. Cook and serve immediately with a little Hollandaise Sauce (see page 47).

PAPILLOTE OF SALMON WITH FRESH HERBS

Per person
**4 oz (110 g) piece of
 fresh salmon
salt**

Herb Butter
**2 oz (55 g/½ stick) butter
4 teaspoons finely chopped and
 mixed fresh parsley, thyme,
 chives, lemon balm and fennel**

**a squeeze of lemon juice
salt and freshly ground pepper**

Salt the salmon well on all sides. Cream the butter and add the finely chopped herbs, a good squeeze of lemon juice and a little freshly ground pepper. Proceed as in the master recipe (see page 47) using a blob of herb butter on each piece of salmon.

Baked Cod Niçoise

T his is an extremely simple fish dish with a rich, robust flavour. Virtually any round fish may be used, and it is just as suitable for a starter as for a main course, but remember to halve the quantities!

**1½ lb (675 g) cod *or* haddock
 fillet, cut into 6 portions
salt and freshly ground pepper
1 lb (450 g) very ripe tomatoes,
 skinned, deseeded, chopped
 and sprinkled with a
 little sugar
1-2 cloves of garlic, crushed
1 tablespoon approx. capers, rinsed
12 black olives, stoned and sliced
2 tablespoons approx. chopped
 fresh parsley**

**1 teaspoon fresh thyme leaves
3 tablespoons (4 American
 tablespoons) extra virgin
 olive oil**

Serves 6 as main course

Preheat the oven to 200°C/400°F /regulo 6. Season the fish with salt and freshly ground pepper. Prepare and mix all the remaining ingredients. Place the fish in a single layer in an oiled ovenproof dish. Spoon over the tomato mixture. Bake in the preheated oven until just cooked through — 15 minutes approx. Serve with a good green salad and some tiny new potatoes.

Pasta

How to cook pasta

ᵛ *Spaghetti with Warm Tomato and Fresh Herb Sauce*

Spaghetti alla Carbonara

Spaghetti alla Puttanesca

* *Pasta Shells with Tomatoes, Spicy Sausage and Cream*

Pasta with Sardines, Pine Kernels and Raisins

ᵛ *Tagliatelle with Cream and Asparagus*

Tagliatelle with Smoked Salmon and Parsley

ᵛ* *Penne with Red and Yellow Peppers and Basil Leaves*

ᵛ *Indian Spicy Noodles with Tomato*

ᵛ* *Macaroni Cheese*

Macaroni Cheese with Smoked Salmon

ᵛ *Macaroni Cheese with Mushrooms and Courgettes*

* *Pasta Salad with Tuna and Beans*

ᵛ *Orzo Salad with Pesto, Cherry Tomatoes*

and Knockalara Cheese

ᵛ* *Orzo with Pesto*

It doesn't seem all that long ago since spaghetti was considered quite exotic, but in the space of just a few years all that has changed. Now pasta is the first thing to spring to mind when time is short in the kitchen. Suddenly we are acquiring the Italian knack of rustling up tasty, colourful concoctions with minimum fuss, all based around the huge variety of twirls, bows, butterflies and quills which have charmed their way on to Irish tables.

If you want to make a meal in minutes, homemade pasta is more or less out of the question. The choice lies between dried pasta and the fresh vacuum-packed type, now increasingly widely available. In both cases, there are good brands and bad, so you may need to buy a few different makes. Do some critical tasting to find the best flavour and texture. As well as straightforward pasta, in an array of colours and shapes, many varieties like stuffed cushions of pasta are beginning to come into the shops. While some of these are delicious, and marvellous for a quick meal, others are not quite what the Italians intended, so conduct a spot of careful research.

Pasta is so incredibly versatile that there is no limit to the number of combinations you can create in a matter of minutes. All you need is a little imagination and flair.

* How to cook pasta

T*he trick when cooking pasta is to use a large amount of water, and not to overcook it. Note that if you are using a recipe which calls for more pasta than this, the amount of water and salt used must be increased proportionately.*

8 oz (225 g) pasta — spaghetti, tagliatelle *or* noodles
4 pints (2.3 L/10 cups) water
2 teaspoons salt

Serves 4

Cook the pasta by putting it into plenty of boiling salted water. Boil for 2 minutes, remove the pan from the heat and cover tightly. Leave the pasta in the water for 12-15 minutes before straining. The exact amount of time will depend on the thickness of the pasta. Test it after 12 minutes. It should be cooked through but still *al dente* — i.e. with a bit of a bite.

Alternatively, boil for the entire time.

SHELLS, PENNE, MACARONI, SPIRALS

C ook as above but boil for 3-4 minutes, depending on size, before turning off the heat.

ᵛ Spaghetti with Warm Tomato and Fresh Herb Sauce

8 oz (225 g) spaghetti *or* tagliatelle
6 tablespoons (8 American tablespoons) extra virgin olive oil
4 cloves of garlic, crushed
6 very ripe tomatoes, seeded and diced
6 sundried tomatoes, chopped
2 tablespoons approx. chopped spring onion, both green and white parts

salt, freshly ground pepper and a good pinch of sugar
2 tablespoons approx. chopped fresh parsley, chives and basil *or* a mixture
a fist of fresh rocket leaves (optional)
freshly grated Parmesan cheese (optional — Parmigiano Reggiano if possible)

51

Serves 4

Cook the pasta in the usual way (see page 51).

Meanwhile make the sauce. Heat the olive oil in a sauté pan, add the garlic and spring onion, stir once or twice, add both sorts of tomatoes, season with salt, freshly ground pepper and sugar, add the herbs and heat until barely warm.

Strain the spaghetti or tagliatelle immediately and serve with the sauce. It's delicious just as it is, but by all means sprinkle a little Parmesan cheese over the top if you wish.

Spaghetti alla Carbonara

F*ast, nutritious, delicious!*

1 lb (450 g) spaghetti
6 oz (170 g) smoked streaky bacon, rindless
4 egg yolks *or* 3 eggs
4 oz (110 g/1 cup) freshly grated Parmesan cheese (Parmigiano Reggiano if possible)
2 fl oz (50 ml) cream
2 cloves of garlic
2 tablespoons extra virgin olive oil
salt and freshly ground pepper
3 fl oz (75 ml) dry white wine (optional)

Garnish
2 tablespoons approx. finely chopped fresh parsley

Serves 8

Cook the pasta in the usual way (see page 51).

While it is cooking, cut the streaky bacon into small strips ½ inch (1 cm) wide. Break eggs into a large bowl and whisk them with the cheese, cream, salt and freshly ground pepper. Peel and crush the garlic and sauté in the olive oil in a non-reactive saucepan until golden, then discard it. Put the bacon into the pan and sauté until it begins to brown, then add the wine if using and let it simmer for a few minutes.

When the pasta is *al dente* drain well. While still very hot, add to the bowl with the eggs so that the heat of the pasta cooks the eggs. Toss rapidly. Add the sizzling bacon and olive oil and toss again thoroughly. Serve sprinkled with parsley.

Spaghetti alla Puttanesca

*L*iterally translated, this means whore's pasta — in other words it's hot stuff with a good gutsy flavour!

8 oz (225 g) spaghetti
3 tablespoons (4 American
    tablespoons) extra virgin
    olive oil
2 cloves of garlic, crushed
5 anchovy fillets, chopped
1 × 14 oz (400 g) tin
    tomatoes, chopped
salt, freshly ground pepper
    and sugar
1 teaspoon chopped fresh annual
    marjoram *or* oregano
1 tablespoon approx. capers
8 black olives, stoned and cut
    into slices

Serves 4

Cook the pasta in the usual way (see page 51).

While it is cooking, make the sauce. Warm the olive oil in a large sauté pan, add the garlic and anchovies and cook for a few minutes over a low heat until the anchovies dissolve. Increase the heat and add the chopped tomatoes with their juice, season with salt, freshly ground pepper and a good pinch of sugar. Bring to the boil and simmer until the tomatoes have reduced to a thickish sauce — 10 minutes approx.

Add the marjoram, capers and olives. When the pasta is *al dente* drain well and toss with the sauce over a low heat.

Taste and correct the seasoning, turn into a hot pasta dish and serve at once.

* Pasta Shells with Tomatoes, Spicy Sausage and Cream

*A*robust sauce with plenty of flavour.

1 lb (450 g) pasta shells
1 oz (30 g/¼ stick) butter
2 tablespoons approx.
    chopped scallion
1 teaspoon finely chopped
    fresh rosemary
1½ lb (675 g) fresh ripe tomatoes,
    peeled, seeded and cut into

½-inch (1 cm) dice
    or 1½ × 14 oz (400 g) tins
    chopped tomatoes
8 oz (225 g) chorizo *or* kabanossi
    sausage, sliced
a pinch of crushed chillies
salt and freshly ground pepper
4 fl oz (120 ml/½ cup) cream
1 tablespoon approx. fresh
    finely chopped flat parsley

4 tablespoons (5 generous American tablespoons) freshly grated Parmesan cheese (Parmigiano Reggiano if possible)

Serves 6

Cook the pasta in the usual way (see page 51).

While it is cooking, make the sauce. Melt the butter in a large sauté pan, add the scallion and cook over a gentle heat for a few minutes until lightly browned. Add the rosemary, tomatoes and sausage to the pan.

Cook until the tomatoes begin to soften — 5 minutes approx. Add the crushed chillies to the sauce mixture in the sauté pan and season lightly with salt and freshly ground pepper (be careful not to overdo the salt as the sausage may be quite salty). Add the cream and chopped parsley and allow to bubble, stirring frequently until the cream has reduced by about half.

When the pasta is *al dente,* drain and toss with the sauce, add the Parmesan cheese and toss again.Check the seasoning and serve at once.

Pasta with Sardines, Pine Kernels and Raisins

Purists would be very sniffy about my use of canned rather than fresh sardines in this classic Sicilian dish. However, I make no apologies: it tastes delicious — and anyway, fresh sardines are thin on the ground in Ballycotton, not to speak of Cullohill!

12 oz (340 g) spaghetti
**   *or* tagliatelle**
2 tins best quality sardines
**   preserved in olive oil**
2 tablespoons (2 generous American tablespoons) extra virgin olive oil
4 oz (110 g/scant 1 cup) chopped onion
2 oz (55 g/1 cup) pine kernels, lightly toasted
2 oz (55 g) raisins, plumped up in hot water

2-4 tablespoons (2½-5 American tablespoons) chopped fennel leaves
6 tablespoons (8 American tablespoons) fine dried breadcrumbs *or* 3 tablespoons (4 American tablespoons) grated Parmesan cheese★

Serves 6

★ *Dried toasted breadcrumbs were the poor man's Parmesan in Sicily.*

Cook the pasta in the usual way (see page 51).

Heat the olive oil in a sauté pan, add the onion and cook on a gentle heat until soft and golden. Add the toasted pine kernels, raisins and fennel and toss well. When the pasta is almost cooked, add the sardines to the sauce.

Drain the pasta, drizzle with a little extra virgin olive oil, add the sardine mixture and toss gently. Taste and correct the seasoning.

Turn into a hot serving dish and serve immediately sprinkled with dried breadcrumbs or grated Parmesan cheese.

ᵛ Tagliatelle with Cream and Asparagus

W ickedly rich but utterly delicious once a year.

8 oz (225 g) tagliatelle
8 oz (225 g) fresh Irish asparagus
salt
1 oz (30 g/¼ stick) butter
6 oz (170 g/¾ cup) best
   quality cream
2 oz (55 g/½ cup) freshly grated
   Parmesan cheese (Parmigiano
   Reggiano if possible)
freshly ground pepper, sea salt
   and nutmeg

Serves 4 as a main course, 8 as a starter

Snap off the root end of the asparagus where it breaks naturally, cook the asparagus in boiling salted water until al dente, drain and save.

Cook the pasta in the usual way (see page 51).

Cut the asparagus into thin slices at an angle, no thicker than ¼ inch (5 mm). Melt the butter in a wide saucepan, add half the cream and simmer for a couple of minutes until the cream thickens slightly. Add the asparagus, the hot drained tagliatelle, the rest of the cream and the Parmesan cheese. Season with freshly ground pepper, sea salt and nutmeg. Toss briefly — just enough to coat the pasta — taste and add a little more seasoning if necessary. Serve immediately.

TAGLIATELLE WITH SMOKED SALMON AND PARSLEY

O mit the asparagus from the above recipe. Substitute 4-8 oz (110-225 g) smoked salmon, cut into cubes, and 2 tablespoons approx. of chopped fresh parsley. Omit the Parmesan cheese. Serve immediately.

v* Penne with Red and Yellow Peppers and Basil Leaves

12 oz (340 g/4 cups) penne
3 each fleshy red and yellow
    peppers (Spanish if possible)
4 tablespoons (5 generous
    American tablespoons)
    extra virgin olive oil
3-4 cloves of garlic, crushed
salt and freshly cracked pepper
2 oz (55 g/½ stick) butter
20 large fresh basil leaves
4 oz (110 g/1 cup) freshly
    grated Parmesan cheese
    (Parmigiano Reggiano
    if possible)

Serves 6

Cook the pasta in the usual way (see page 51).

While it is cooking, cut the peppers into quarters, deseed them and cut into strips 1 inch (2.5 cm) wide approx. Heat the olive oil in a wide sauté pan and add the garlic. Cook for 1-2 minutes and add the peppers. Toss, cover the pan and cook for 10 minutes approx., stirring every now and then. They should hold their shape but be tender and sweet. Season well with salt and freshly cracked pepper.

When the pasta is *al dente*, drain it, put into a hot serving dish and toss with a little olive oil. Add the butter to the peppers, pour over the pasta, add the torn basil leaves and the Parmesan cheese. Toss and serve immediately on very hot plates.

v Indian Spicy Noodles with Tomato

T*his vegetarian noodle dish is so filling that you wouldn't even notice the absence of meat. Whip up this addictive dish with a packet of those crispy noodles from your store cupboard.*

4 oz (110 g) egg noodles, cooked
3 tablespoons (4 American
    tablespoons) peanut *or*
    sunflower oil
½ teaspoon cumin seeds
5 cloves of garlic, finely chopped
1 green chilli, deseeded and
    finely chopped

1-inch (2.5 cm) piece of fresh
    root ginger
a good pinch of ground asafoetida
    (optional — see glossary)
¼ teaspoon ground turmeric
¼-½ teaspoon cayenne pepper
4 oz (110 g/scant 1 cup)
    onion, chopped
6 ripe tomatoes, peeled and
    coarsely chopped
¾ teaspoon salt
freshly ground pepper
½ teaspoon sugar

**3 tablespoons (4 American
  tablespoons) finely chopped
  fresh coriander**

Garnish
chopped fresh coriander

Serves 4-6

Heat the oil in a wok or large frying pan (preferably non-stick) over a medium heat. When hot, add the cumin seeds. Let them sizzle for 10 seconds. Add the garlic, chilli and ginger which should be peeled, finely sliced and then very finely chopped. Stir and fry for 2-3 minutes or until

the garlic begins to turn light brown.

Add the asafetida, turmeric and cayenne pepper. Stir very quickly, then add the onion and cook for 3-4 minutes on a medium heat. Toss in the tomatoes, season with salt, freshly ground pepper and sugar and cook for 5-6 minutes, stirring frequently. Add the coriander and simmer for 2-3 minutes more, or until the tomatoes are tender.

Stir the cooked noodles into the tomato mixture. Bubble for 1-2 minutes to heat the noodles through. Serve immediately with lots of fresh coriander.

ᵛ* Macaroni Cheese

A lthough Macaroni Cheese reheats perfectly, I love it just as soon as the pasta has been mixed with the creamy sauce. It is incredibly versatile. Mix some tasty bits through it, layer it with little chunks of salami, smoked salmon or chargrilled vegetables. When it comes to serving, forget the old Pyrex and use a really stylish ovenproof dish. Macaroni Cheese needs a new image!

8 oz (225 g/2½ cups) macaroni
2 oz (55 g/½ stick) butter
**2 oz (55 g/½ cup) white flour,
  unbleached if possible**
**1½ pints (900 ml/3¾ cups)
  boiling milk**
¼ teaspoon Dijon mustard
1 tablespoon approx. chopped

fresh parsley (optional)
**5 oz (140 g/1¼ cups) grated
  mature Cheddar cheese**
salt and freshly ground pepper

pie dish, 2 pint (1.1 L) capacity

Serves 6

Cook the macaroni in the usual way for pasta (see page 51), stirring when you drop it into the boiling water to make sure it doesn't stick together. When it is just soft, drain well.

Meanwhile melt the butter, add in the flour and cook, stirring occasionally, for 1-2 minutes. Remove from the heat. Whisk in the milk gradually, then bring to the boil, stirring all the time. Add the mustard, parsley if used and cheese, and season with salt and freshly ground pepper to taste. Add in the cooked macaroni, bring back to the boil and serve immediately.

Macaroni Cheese reheats very successfully provided the pasta is not overcooked in the first place. It is very good served with cold meat, particularly ham.

MACARONI CHEESE WITH SMOKED SALMON

S tir 4 oz (110 g) of chopped smoked salmon through the

Macaroni Cheese just before serving.

ᵛ MACARONI CHEESE WITH MUSHROOMS AND COURGETTES

L ayer the Macaroni Cheese with 8 oz (225 g) sliced sautéed mushrooms and 8 oz (225 g) sliced courgettes cooked in olive oil with a

little garlic and marjoram or basil. Scatter the top with grated cheese. Reheat and flash under a grill if necessary.

OTHER VARIATIONS

M acaroni Cheese is also pretty irresistible with a layer of
Tomato Fondue (see page 101)
and Bacon
Mushroom à la Crème
(see page 102)

Mushroom à la Crème
with Shrimps and Mussels
Piperonata (see page 103)
and Salami

* Pasta Salad with Tuna and Beans

A *few tins of cooked beans are an invaluable standby for instant salads and vegetable dishes. In this substantial main course salad, it is*

important that the cooked pasta be soaked in French Dressing while it is still warm so that it absorbs extra flavour.

4 oz (110 g/1⅓ cups) pasta shells
   or penne
7 oz (200 g) tinned
   black-eyed beans
7 oz (200 g) tinned haricot beans
7 oz (200 g) tinned red
   kidney beans
salt and freshly ground
   black pepper
¼ pint (150 ml/generous ½ cup)
   French Dressing (see page 93)
2 tablespoons approx. spring
   onion, chopped diagonally
1 tablespoon approx. chopped
   fresh chives
1 tablespoon approx. finely
   chopped fresh parsley
a few fresh rocket leaves
   if available
1 × 7 oz (200 g) tin tuna fish
   (dolphin-friendly), drained
16 small black Niçoise olives
freshly squeezed lemon juice

Serves 8

Cook the pasta in the usual way (see page 51). Warm the beans, season with salt and freshly ground pepper and toss in some French Dressing immediately. Drain the pasta, toss in some of the French Dressing while still warm and season well.

Mix the pasta with the beans, spring onion, half the chives and parsley and a few rocket leaves if you have them. Add the tuna and gently mix so as not to break up the flesh too much. Taste for seasoning, add a little more French Dressing and some freshly squeezed lemon juice if necessary.

Pile into a serving dish and scatter over the remaining herbs and the black olives.

ᵛ Orzo Salad with Pesto, Cherry Tomatoes and Knockalara Cheese

O rzo is one of my best discoveries in recent years. Essentially it is pasta grains, which may be used in a whole variety of dishes both hot and cold. For this salad we normally use Knockalara cheese, made from ewe's milk in Cappoquin, Co. Waterford — but you could use Feta cheese instead.

8 oz (225 g/3 cups) Orzo
2 tablespoons Pesto
   (see page 60)

12 cherry tomatoes,
   red and yellow mixed
   if possible
salt and freshly ground pepper
balsamic vinegar
   or red wine vinegar
a pinch of sugar
1 oz (30 g) toasted pine kernels
3 oz (85 g) Knockalara
   or Feta cheese cut
   into ¾ inch
   (2 cm) cubes

Garnish
rocket leaves if available
sprigs of basil

Serves 4-6

Cook the Orzo following the normal pasta method (see page 51) until *al dente*. Drain, rinse quickly under the tap and allow to cool. Put into a large bowl and toss with the Pesto.

Quarter the tomatoes, and season with salt and freshly ground pepper. Sprinkle with balsamic or red wine vinegar and sugar and toss well. Toast the pine kernels until golden.

Add the tomatoes and pine kernels to the Orzo which should by now be cool. Toss gently. Add the cubes of cheese and toss one more time. Turn on to a serving dish, and garnish the top with rocket leaves and perhaps a sprig or two of basil.

Eat immediately.

v* Orzo with Pesto

8 oz (225 g/3 cups) Orzo (pasta grains — see previous recipe)
olive oil
2-3 tablespoons (2½-4 American tablespoons) Pesto (see below)

Serves 4-6

Cook the Orzo following the normal pasta method (see page 51) until *al dente*. Drain, rinse quickly under the tap and allow to cool.

Put into a large bowl and toss with the Pesto. Serve immediately.

PESTO

*H*omemade pesto takes minutes to make and tastes infinitely better than most of what you buy. The problem is getting enough basil. If you have difficulty, use parsley or a mixture of parsley and mint — different but still delicious. And do taste the pine kernels when you buy them, to make sure they are not rancid.

4 oz (110 g) fresh basil leaves
5 fl oz (150 ml/generous ½ cup) extra virgin olive oil
1 oz (30 g) fresh pine kernels
2 large cloves of garlic, peeled and crushed
2 oz (55 g/½ cup) finely grated
fresh Parmesan cheese (Parmigiano Reggiano if possible)
salt to taste

Using a food processor or a pestle and mortar, whizz or pound the basil with the olive oil, pine kernels and garlic. Remove to a bowl and fold in the Parmesan cheese. Taste and season.

Pesto keeps for weeks, covered with a layer of olive oil in a jar in the fridge. It also freezes well, but for best results don't add the grated Parmesan until it has defrosted. Freeze it in small jars for convenience.

Grains and Pulses

*v** How to boil rice to perfection*
* Pilaff Rice
Pilaff with Fresh Herbs
Pilaff with Mussels and Prawns
* Fried Rice
vv Couscous with Apricots and Toasted Almonds
vv* Tabouleh
vv Claudia Roden's Hummus bi Tahina
Lentils with Bacon

This may not sound the most exciting section, but grains and pulses earn their place in a book on meals in minutes for a whole host of reasons. To begin with, many of them are really quick to prepare. Some, like bulgar and couscous, don't even need to be cooked; soaking is all that is required. Many, ounce for ounce, are more nutritious than almost any other food you can think of, besides being incredibly inexpensive. Furthermore, I have to tell you that grains and pulses have become frightfully fashionable. No trendy menu is complete these days without its complement of lentils, couscous and chickpeas.

The normal procedure of soaking and boiling dried beans puts them beyond the time limit of the recipes in this book, but tinned beans of all kinds are a terrific store cupboard stand-by. Kidney beans, chickpeas, haricot beans and black-eye beans can form the basis of all sorts of delicious dishes in a matter of minutes. These, with the various grains I have mentioned, constitute a whole category of interesting, enormously versatile foods which too many people completely ignore. Do rummage for them on the shelves of your local health food shops and delicatessens, and find out what you have been missing!

v* How to boil rice to perfection

See the recipe for Fluffy White Rice on page 31.

* Pilaff Rice

Although a risotto can be made in 20 minutes, it entails 20 minutes of pretty constant stirring which makes it feel rather laboursome. A pilaff, on the other hand, looks after itself once the initial cooking is underway. It is immensely versatile — you can serve it as a plain accompaniment or add whatever tasty bits you have to hand to make a complete meal. Beware, however, of using pilaff as a dustbin. All additions should be carefully seasoned and balanced.

**14 oz (400 g/2 cups) long-grain
  rice (Basmati if possible)
1 oz (30 g/¼ stick) butter
2 tablespoons finely chopped
  onion *or* shallot
salt and freshly ground pepper
32 fl oz (975 ml/4 cups)**

**homemade fish, chicken
or vegetable stock**

Serves 8

Melt the butter in a casserole, add the onion and sweat for 2-3 minutes. Add the rice and toss for 1-2 minutes — just long enough for the grains to change colour. Add salt and freshly ground pepper, pour in the stock, cover and bring to the boil.

Simmer either on top of the stove or in the oven for 10 minutes approx. By then the rice should have absorbed all the liquid and be just cooked. Serve in a warm dish.

Note: Basmati rice cooks quite quickly; other types may take up to 15 minutes.

PILAFF WITH FRESH HERBS

Stir in 2 tablespoons approx. chopped fresh herbs — parsley, thyme or chives, just before serving.

Pilaff with Mussels and Prawns

**1 quantity basic Pilaff
  recipe above
1 lb (450 g) mussels
1 quantity Mushroom à la Crème
  (see page 102)
¼ lb (110 g) cooked shrimps
  or prawns**

Garnish
**1-2 tablespoons chopped
  fresh herbs — parsley,
  chives, thyme, fennel**

Prepare the pilaff in the usual way, using fish stock if possible.

Wash the mussels in several changes of cold water. Put them into a wide frying or sauté pan in a single layer on a medium heat. Cover with a lid or folded tea towel. As soon as the mussels open, whip them out, remove the beards and discard the shells.

Heat the Mushroom à la Crème and stir in the mussels and shrimps. When the pilaff is cooked, turn into a hot serving dish, then spoon the mushroom and shellfish mixture over the top. Sprinkle with chopped herbs and serve immediately.

OTHER GOOD THINGS TO ADD TO PILAFF

Cubes of cooked ham, bacon or chicken

sautéed mushrooms

* Fried Rice

Fried Rice is a terrific and very nutritious way of using up leftovers. It can be ready to eat in just a few minutes. There are at least half a dozen variations of fried rice in China. Some people like to add the eggs to the wok first, followed by the rice. My family favour adding the egg at the later stage for a more moist result. Other tasty bits, e.g. bamboo shoots, bean sprouts and Chinese mushrooms, may be added.

1 lb (450 g) cooked rice (see page 31)
2 eggs, lightly beaten
4 tablespoons (5–6 American tablespoons) chopped spring onion, both green and white parts
1 teaspoon salt
3 tablespoons (4 American tablespoons) sunflower or extra virgin olive oil
4 oz (110 g/1¼ cups) mushrooms, chopped
4 oz (110 g) cooked meat (chicken, pork, ham or spicy sausage) cut into small dice or 4 oz (110 g) peeled prawns or shrimps
4 oz (110 g) cooked green peas or green pepper
1-2 tablespoons (1½-2½ American tablespoons) light soy sauce

Serves 6

Whisk the eggs with half the chopped spring onion and the salt.

Heat the oil in a very hot wok, add the mushrooms, stir-fry for 1-2 minutes, then add the meat or shrimps, peas and remaining spring onion. Continue to stir-fry for a further 1-2 minutes. Add the rice and soy sauce, continue to stir-fry, add the eggs and stir fry for 2 minutes approx., until they are set. Stir to make sure that each grain of rice is separate. Taste, correct the seasoning and serve immediately.

ᵛᵛ Couscous with Apricots and Toasted Almonds

Couscous may be served absolutely plain as a delicious staple to soak up the juices of a flavourful stew.

12 oz (340 g/scant 2 cups) couscous
2 oz (55 g/⅓ cup) dried apricots, soaked in cold water
2 oz (55 g/½ cup) toasted split almonds
salt and freshly ground pepper
4 tablespoons (5 generous American tablespoons) extra virgin olive oil

Serves 8
Cover the couscous in its own volume of water and allow to soak for 15 minutes, stirring every now and then. Chop the apricots and add to the couscous with the almonds. Put into a thick covered dish and heat through in a moderate oven for 20 minutes approx., or alternatively steam over simmering water or stock. Season with salt and freshly ground pepper and add the olive oil.

Variation: Instead of apricots and almonds, stir in 2 tablespoons of chopped fresh herbs just before serving, e.g. mint or coriander, parsley and chives.

Pangrilled Chicken Breasts with Couscous, Raisins and Pistachio Nuts

See page 21.

ᵛᵛ* Tabouleh

This refreshing and highly nutritious Middle Eastern salad which sustained hardworking peasants for generations is now found on fancy restaurant menus. It can be served as a starter or main dish.

4 oz (110 g/¾ cup) bulgar (cracked wheat)
3 fl oz (75 ml) extra virgin olive oil
freshly squeezed juice of 1-2 lemons

salt and freshly ground pepper

4 tablespoons approx. chopped fresh parsley

2 tablespoons approx. chopped fresh mint

4 tablespoons approx. chopped spring onion, both green and white parts

Garnish

small crisp lettuce leaves — cos *or* iceberg

6 very ripe firm tomatoes, seeded, diced and sprinkled with a little salt, freshly ground pepper and sugar

1 firm crisp cucumber, finely diced

sprigs of flat parsley

black olives (optional)

Accompaniment
pitta bread

Serves 6-12, depending on whether it is a starter or main course

Soak the bulgar in 8 fl oz (250 ml/1 cup) cold water for 30 minutes approx., drain and squeeze well to remove any excess liquid. Stir in the olive oil and some of the freshly squeezed lemon juice. Season with salt and freshly ground pepper and leave aside to absorb the dressing while you chop the parsley, mint and spring onion. Just before serving, mix the herbs with the bulgar, taste and add more lemon juice if necessary. It should have a fresh and lively flavour.

Arrange the Tabouleh on a serving plate surrounded by lettuce leaves and little mounds of well seasoned tomato and cucumber dice. Garnish with sprigs of flat parsley, and a few black olives if you like them. Warm pitta bread is the perfect accompaniment.

ᵛᵛ Claudia Roden's Hummus bi Tahina

Hummus bi Tahina with its rich, earthy taste has quite a cult following. Although it may seem strange at first, the flavour soon grows on you. It makes an excellent starter served as a dip with pitta bread. It is also delicious with kebabs or as a salad with a main dish, and has a particular affinity with aubergines. Tahina paste is available from health food shops and delicatessens.

4-6 oz (110-170 g/¾-1¼ cups) chickpeas, cooked

(use tinned to save time)

freshly squeezed juice of 2-3 lemons

2-3 cloves of garlic, crushed

5 fl oz (150 ml/generous ½ cup) tahina paste

salt

Garnish

1 teaspoon paprika

1 tablespoon extra virgin olive oil

1 tablespoon approx. finely chopped fresh parsley

cumin (optional)
a few cooked chickpeas

Accompaniment
**pitta bread *or* any crusty
white bread**

Serves 4-8, depending on how it is used

Drain the chickpeas and keep a few whole ones aside for garnish. Whizz up the remainder in an electric mixer or blender or food processor with the lemon juice, the crushed garlic, tahina paste and salt to taste. Blend to a soft, creamy paste, tasting and adding lemon juice, more salt and a little water if necessary, until you are happy with the flavour and consistency.

Pour the mixture into a serving dish. Mix the paprika with the olive oil and dribble over the surface in a cross. Do the same with the chopped parsley. Cumin is also a delicious addition. Sprinkle with the reserved chickpeas.

Lentils with Bacon

T*he little green speckled Du Puy lentils are the aristocrats of the lentil family, and they cook in no time at all. Serve them just as a vegetable with a crispy duck breast, or stir in some pieces of cooked ham or bacon and a few cubes of golden delicious apple sautéed in butter for a complete meal.*

**½ lb (225 g/1 generous cup)
Du Puy lentils
2-4 oz (55-110 g) cooked
bacon, cubed
1 carrot
1 onion stuck with 2 cloves
bouquet garni
butter *or* extra virgin olive oil
lots of freshly squeezed
lemon juice
2 tablespoons approx. chopped
fresh herbs — fresh oregano,
annual marjoram *or* parsley
sea salt and freshly
ground pepper**

Serves 4-6

Wash the lentils and put them into a large saucepan. Fill with cold water, add the carrot, onion and bouquet garni and bring slowly to the boil. Reduce the heat and simmer very gently for 15-20 minutes, testing regularly. The lentils should be *al dente* (with a little bite in them) but not hard. Drain, remove and discard the carrot, onion and bouquet garni. Season the lentils while warm with a good knob of butter or some extra virgin olive oil, then add lots of freshly squeezed lemon juice, the herbs and the cubes of freshly cooked bacon. Season with sea salt and freshly ground pepper. Serve immediately.

Note: Lentils are also good with a little finely chopped chilli added. Half a small chilli with seeds removed would be about right.

Egg and Cheese Dishes

v* *Boiled Eggs with Soldiers and Asparagus*
v* *Perfect Poached Eggs on Toast*
v* *Buttered Eggs*
v* *Scrambled Eggs*
* *Scrambled Eggs with Smoked Salmon*
v *Scrambled Eggs with Tomato*
v *Scrambled Eggs with Tarragon and Basil*
v *Scrambled Eggs with Chives*
v *Scrambled Eggs with Asparagus*
Scrambled Eggs with Smoked Bacon
v* *Mexican Scrambled Eggs*
v *Indian Scrambled Eggs*
v *French Omelette*
* *Californian Omelette Sandwich*
v* *Frittata*
Fluffy Savoury Omelette
v *Ballymaloe Cheese Fondue*

No matter how bare the cupboard may be, there are usually some eggs and a bit of cheese to spare. Very few other foods can provide such a sustaining meal so quickly. A couple of eggs, boiled or scrambled, will satisfy even the most ravenous appetite.

However, the quality of the eggs is all-important to the flavour of the dish. For years I have extolled the virtues of free-range eggs. I cannot imagine life without a few hens of my own, but I realise this is not a practical proposition for a great many people. The next best thing is to seek out good free-range eggs in the supermarket, or better still, buy directly from a farm if you happen to be in the country. Be willing to pay a little extra, because true free-range eggs are produced in smaller quantities than battery eggs — and remember that the extra investment will be more than repaid in the superb flavour and texture of the genuine article. Really good eggs are a gourmet treat, special enough to be served unadorned, and with pride.

It is important to realise that

although they are wonderful foods, eggs and many cheeses are high in cholesterol. People with heart problems should be careful not to over-indulge, no matter how delicious they may be.

ᵛ* Boiled Eggs with Soldiers and Asparagus

Those of us who are fortunate enough to have some space to keep a few free-range hens are blessed indeed. The eggs laid by my happy, lazy hens are completely perfect — white curdy albumen and rich yellow yolks. When you have access to eggs of this quality, treat yourself to a boiled egg — absolute perfection but sadly a forgotten flavour for so many people. Little fingers of toast called dippies or soldiers are the usual accessory, but during the asparagus season in May a few spears of fresh green asparagus make a deliciously decadent dip.

**2 fresh eggs, free-range
— in fact, if you don't have
a free-range egg, forget
the whole idea and cook
something else
6-8 spears of fresh
Irish asparagus
1 slice fresh white pan loaf
a few pats of butter
salt and freshly ground pepper**

Serves 2

Bring a small saucepan of water to the boil, gently slide in the eggs, bring the water back to the boil and simmer gently for 4-6 minutes, according to your taste. A 4-minute egg will be still quite soft; 5 minutes will almost set the white while the yolk will still be runny; and 6 minutes will produce a boiled egg with a soft yolk and solid white.

Trim the stalks of the asparagus, and cook in boiling salted water for 7-8 minutes or until a knife will pierce the root end easily. Drain and keep hot.

While the asparagus is cooking, toast the bread, cut off the crusts and spread with butter. Cut into fingers. As soon as the eggs are cooked, pop them into egg cups on large side plates. Put the cooked asparagus and soldiers on the side and serve with a pepper mill, sea salt and a few pats of butter.

ᵛ* Perfect Poached Eggs on Toast

No fancy egg poachers or moulds are needed to produce a perfect

result — simply a really fresh egg laid by a happy hen!

2 eggs, free-range if possible
toast, freshly made from a
slice of pan loaf

Serves 1

Bring a small saucepan of water to the boil, reduce the heat, swirl the water, crack the egg and slip gently into the whirlpool in the centre. For perfection the water should not boil again but bubble very gently just below boiling point. Continue to cook for 3-4 minutes until the white is set and the yolk still soft and runny.

Meanwhile make a slice of toast, cut off the crusts, butter and pop on to a hot plate. Drain the poached egg or eggs and place on top. Serve immediately.

Note: Poached eggs are also delicious served on a bed of creamy spinach nicely flavoured with nutmeg, or on top of Piperonata (see page 103).

^{v*} Buttered Eggs

This oldfashioned way of preserving eggs in the short term is only possible if you have your own hens. It is still traditional in my part of the country. Buttered eggs can be found in the Old English Market in Cork City.

Take the eggs warm from the nest. Rub the shells all over with a tiny scrap of butter to seal the pores. Store the eggs in a cool place. Not only will they keep for several weeks, but the albumen will have a wonderful curdy texture reminiscent of a newly laid egg.

^{v*} Scrambled Eggs

Perfectly scrambled eggs are rare indeed. I've had some positively horrendous concoctions served up for breakfast in some posh hotels. On one particularly memorable occasion they arrived in a solid mound garnished with a sprig of redcurrants! Really fresh eggs, perfectly scrambled, need no further embellishment, except perhaps a slice of hot, thin toast.

4 eggs, free-range if possible
2 tablespoons approx.
creamy milk
a knob of butter
salt and freshly ground pepper

Serves 2

69

Break the eggs into a bowl, add the milk and season with salt and freshly ground pepper. Whisk well until the whites and yolks are well mixed. Put a blob of butter into a cold saucepan, pour in the egg mixture and stir continuously over a low heat until the eggs have scrambled into soft creamy curds. Serve immediately on warm plates with lots of hot buttered toast or fresh soda bread.

Note: If the plates are too hot the scrambled egg can actually overcook between the stove and the table.

* SCRAMBLED EGGS WITH SMOKED SALMON

Some hotels serve it for breakfast but I rather prefer it for supper on a tray beside the fire. A few seconds before the scrambled egg is fully cooked, add 2-3 tablespoons of diced smoked salmon trimmings, stir once or twice, sprinkle with a little chopped parsley and serve immediately.

ᵛ SCRAMBLED EGGS WITH TOMATO

A few seconds before the scrambled egg is fully cooked, add 1 very ripe chopped tomato which has been seasoned with salt, freshly ground pepper and sugar, stir once or twice and serve immediately.

ᵛ SCRAMBLED EGGS WITH TARRAGON AND BASIL

Add 1 teaspoon of chopped fresh tarragon and basil a few seconds before the end of the cooking time and serve immediately.

ᵛ SCRAMBLED EGGS WITH CHIVES

Add 1-2 teaspoons of chopped fresh chives a few seconds before the end of the cooking time. Cold scrambled egg with chives make *the* best egg sandwiches.

ᵛ SCRAMBLED EGGS WITH ASPARAGUS

Add 2-4 stalks of freshly cooked asparagus cut into diagonal slices a few seconds before the end of the cooking time.

SCRAMBLED EGGS WITH SMOKED BACON

Cook 2-3 tablespoons of bacon dice in 1 tablespoon of extra virgin olive oil until crisp and golden. Add to the scrambled egg with 2 teaspoons of chopped fresh parsley a few seconds before the end of the cooking time and serve immediately.

v* Mexican Scrambled Eggs — Huevos a la Mexicana

Cholita Diaz, a wonderful Oaxacan cook, showed me how to make this favourite Mexican breakfast dish. One mouthful transports me back to Oaxaca — one of the most magical places in the entire world.

8 eggs, free-range if possible
1½ oz (45 g/⅜ stick) butter (in Oaxaca they would use lard)
1 small onion, finely chopped
1-3 chillies, deseeded and finely chopped (the amount depends on how much excitement you would like in your life!)
1 very ripe tomato, chopped
½ teaspoon salt

Serves 4

Melt the butter in a heavy-bottomed saucepan over a medium heat, cook the onion and chillies until the onion is soft but not coloured, add the tomato and cook gently for a few more minutes.

Meanwhile, whisk the eggs and salt well, add them to the saucepan and scramble, stirring all the time until cooked to your taste. Serve immediately on warm plates, preferably with tortillas.

v Indian Scrambled Eggs

6 large eggs, free-range if possible
3 tablespoons (4 American tablespoons) butter
1 small onion, peeled and finely chopped
½ teaspoon fresh ginger, peeled and very finely grated
½-1 fresh, hot green chilli, deseeded and finely chopped
1 tablespoon chopped fresh green coriander
⅛ teaspoon ground turmeric
½ teaspoon ground cumin
1 very ripe tomato, peeled and chopped
salt and freshly ground pepper

Serves 4

Melt the butter in a medium sized frying pan, preferably non-stick, over a medium heat. Sauté the onion until soft. Add the ginger, chilli, coriander, turmeric, cumin and tomato. Stir and cook for 3-4 minutes or until the tomato softens slightly. Whisk the eggs well, season with salt and freshly ground pepper, add to the pan and stir gently over a medium heat until they form soft, thick curds. Serve immediately on warm plates with Naan bread or toast.

Inspired by a recipe from Madhur Jaffrey's *Illustrated Indian Cookery*.

ᵛ French Omelette

An omelette is the ultimate instant food but many a travesty is served in its name. The whole secret is to have the pan hot enough and to use clarified butter if at all possible. Ordinary butter will burn if your pan is as hot as it ought to be. The omelette should be made in half the time it takes to read this recipe. Your first may not be a joy to behold but persevere — practice makes perfect!

2 eggs, free-range if possible
1 dessertspoon (2 American
teaspoons) water *or* milk
salt and freshly ground pepper
1 dessertspoon (2 American
teaspoons) clarified butter
(see below) *or* extra virgin
olive oil

omelette pan, 9 inch (23 cm)
diameter, non-stick
if possible

Serves 1

Warm a plate in the oven. Whisk the eggs with the water or milk in a bowl with a fork or egg whisk, until thoroughly mixed but not too fluffy. Season with salt and freshly ground pepper. Put the warm plate beside the cooker.

Heat the omelette pan over a high heat, add the clarified butter and as soon as it sizzles, pour in the egg mixture. It will start to cook immediately, so quickly pull the edges of the omelette towards the centre with a metal or plastic spatula, tilting the pan so that the uncooked egg runs to the sides. Continue until most of the egg is set and will not run any more, then leave the omelette to cook for a further 10 seconds to brown the bottom. If you are using a filling, spoon the hot mixture in a line along the centre at this point.

To fold the omelette: Flip the edge just below the handle of the pan into the centre, then hold the pan almost perpendicular over the plate so that the omelette will flip over again, then half roll, half slide the omelette on to the plate so that it lands folded in three. (It should not take more than 30 seconds in all to make the omelette — perhaps 45 if you are adding a filling.) Serve immediately.

CLARIFIED BUTTER
Melt 8 oz (225 g/2 sticks) butter gently in a saucepan or in the oven. Allow it to stand for a few minutes, then spoon the crusty white layer of salt particles off the top. Underneath this crust there is a clear liquid — clarified butter. The milky liquid at the bottom can be discarded or used in a white sauce.

Clarified butter is excellent for cooking because it can withstand a higher temperature when the salt and milk particles are removed. It will keep, covered, in a fridge for several weeks.

Tomato Fondue (see page 101) with *or* without Pesto (see page 60)

Piperonata (see page 103)

Mushroom à la Crème (see page102)

Fresh herbs: Add 1 teaspoon each of chopped fresh parsley, chives, chervil and tarragon to the eggs just before cooking.

Crispy bacon *or* diced cooked ham

Goat's cheese, Cheddar, Gruyère, Parmesan or a mixture

Kidney: Cook 1 cleaned and diced lamb's kidney gently in a little butter, add 1 teaspoon of chopped fresh parsley and use as a filling.

Smoked salmon or smoked mackerel: Add 1 oz (30 g) approx. fish and perhaps a little finely chopped fresh parsley or dill.

* Californian Omelette Sandwich

This recipe is inspired by some of the great sandwiches I came across on the West Coast of America. I use a delicious loaf made by a local baker — Harringtons in Youghal, Co. Cork — but obviously you can adapt to the bread available in your area. I particularly love this recipe because it tastes great, only takes a few minutes to make and feeds the entire family. Vary the filling to your heart's content.

5 eggs, free-range if possible
1 round, flat crusty white
    loaf of bread
    (1½ lb/675 g approx.)
Pesto (optional — see page 60)
3 tablespoons (4 American
    tablespoons) extra virgin
    olive oil
3 tablespoons chopped green
    scallion, including tops

8 oz (225 g/4 cups)
    mushrooms sliced
salt and freshly ground pepper
1 tablespoon chopped fresh herbs
    — thyme, chives, chervil,
    tarragon, parsley *or* a mixture
8 slices bacon, cooked until crisp
2 red peppers, roasted, peeled
    and cut into wide strips
    (see page 16 for method)

frying pan, 9 inch (23 cm)
    diameter, non-stick if possible

Serves 4-6

Split the bread horizontally and pull out most of the inside of each half, leaving a shell not more than ½ inch (1 cm) thick. (Save the inside for breadcrumbs.) Spread the base with Pesto if using. Pop into a warm oven to crisp the outside if possible.

Heat 1 tablespoon of the oil over a medium heat in the frying pan. Add the scallion and sweat for a few minutes. Increase the heat, add the mushrooms, season with salt and freshly ground pepper and cook for 3-4 minutes. Cool.

Whisk the eggs, season with salt and freshly ground pepper, then add the chopped herbs and the scallion and mushroom mixture.

Wipe the frying pan clean, add another tablespoon of oil and return it to medium heat. Pour in the egg mixture, spreading the mushrooms evenly in the pan. Cook, stirring until the eggs are just set, almost like the texture of firm scrambled egg.

Slide the omelette off the pan into the bottom of the bread. Top with the warm bacon, the roasted peppers and their juices. Cover with the top of the loaf. Serve immediately. Cut it into quarters or wedges and serve with a good green salad and a few cherry tomatoes.

ᵛ* Frittata

A frittata is an Italian omelette. Unlike its soft and creamy French cousin, a frittata is cooked slowly over a very low heat during which time you can be whipping up a delicious salad to accompany it! It is cooked on both sides and cut into wedges like a piece of cake. This is the basic recipe, flavoured with grated cheese and a generous sprinkling of herbs. Like the omelette, though, it can be filled with almost anything that takes your fancy.

6 large eggs, free-range
    if possible
salt and freshly ground
    black pepper
3 oz (85 g/scant 1 cup) freshly
    grated Gruyère cheese
1 oz (30 g/¼ cup) freshly grated
    Parmesan cheese (Parmigiano
    Reggiano if possible)

2 teaspoons chopped
    fresh parsley
1 teaspoon thyme leaves
1 oz (30 g/¼ stick) butter
1 dessertspoon chopped fresh
    basil *or* marjoram

non-stick frying pan,
    7½ inch (19 cm) bottom,
    9 inch (23 cm) top rim

Accompaniment
green salad
tomato salad

Serves 2-4

Whisk the eggs in a bowl, add the salt, freshly ground pepper, herbs and grated cheese. Melt the butter in the non-stick frying pan. When the butter starts to foam, tip in the eggs.

Turn down the heat as low as it will go. Leave the eggs to cook gently for 12 minutes on a heat diffuser mat, or until the underneath is set. The top should still be slightly runny.

Preheat the grill. Pop the pan under the grill for 1 minute to set but not brown the surface. Slide a palette knife under the frittata to free it from the pan. Slide it on to a warm plate.

Serve cut in wedges with a good green salad and perhaps a tomato salad.

Fluffy Savoury Omelette

This delicious omelette would be very good made with smoked salmon or smoked mackerel instead of the bacon suggested below. A vegetarian version can be made with red or green peppers, tomatoes and aubergine.

3 eggs, free-range if possible
3-4 oz (85-110 g) streaky bacon
1 tablespoon (1 generous
    American tablespoon)
    extra virgin olive oil
2 oz (55 g/1 cup)
    mushrooms, sliced
salt and freshly ground pepper
¼ teaspoon thyme leaves
    (optional)
5-6 tablespoon (6-8 American
    tablespoon) cream
2-3 tablespoon (2-4 American
    tablespoons) freshly grated
    Parmesan cheese
    (Parmigiano Reggiano
    if possible)
1 oz (30 g/¼ stick) butter

Garnish
chopped fresh parsley

Accompaniment
green salad

omelette pan, 10 inch (25.5 cm)
    diameter, non-stick if possible

Serves 1-2 as a main course

Cut the rind off the bacon, cut into ¼ inch (5 mm) lardons and fry in a little oil on a good hot pan until crisp and golden. Remove and drain on kitchen paper. Add the sliced mushrooms to the hot bacon fat. Season with salt and freshly ground pepper and add the thyme leaves if using. Toss over a high heat until the mushrooms are wilted, then add to the bacon.

Separate the eggs, beat the yolks with a tablespoon of the cream and season with salt and freshly ground pepper. Whip the egg whites until stiff. Fold into the yolks with the bacon and mushrooms and add half the Parmesan cheese.

Melt the butter in the omelette pan. Pour the mixture in gently and cook over a medium heat until the base of the omelette is golden. Spoon the remaining cream over the top and sprinkle with the rest of the finely grated Parmesan. Pop under a hot grill for a minute or so until golden and bubbly on top. Slide on to a hot dish, sprinkle with chopped parsley and serve immediately accompanied by a good green salad.

ᵛ Ballymaloe Cheese Fondue

N ow that Ballymaloe Country Relish is available countrywide, Myrtle Allen's Cheese Fondue recipe made from Irish Cheddar cheese can be made any time. It's a great favourite at Ballymaloe and even though it is a meal in itself it may be made in minutes and is loved by adults and children alike. It is great fun for a party because you must kiss the gentleman or lady on your right if you drop your bread into the pot, so choose your spot carefully! A fondue set is obviously an advantage but not essential.

**2 tablespoons approx.
dry white wine**
2 small cloves of garlic, crushed
**2 teaspoons Ballymaloe
Country Relish**
2 teaspoons chopped fresh parsley

**6 oz (170 g/2 cups) grated
mature Cheddar cheese
(we use Mitchelstown)**

Accompaniment
crusty white bread

Serves 2

Put the white wine and the rest of the ingredients into a small saucepan or fondue pot and stir. Just before serving put over a low heat until the cheese melts and begins to bubble. Put the pot over the fondue stove and serve immediately with fresh French bread or cubes of ordinary white bread crisped up in a hot oven. Serve with a glass of wine.

Pancakes, Crumpets and Fritters

*Corn Fritters with Pangrilled Chicken Breasts
and Crispy Bacon*
Toad in the Hole
ᵛ Pancakes
ᵛ Savoury Herb Pancakes
ᵛ Sweet Pancakes
*Buttermilk Pancakes with Crispy Bacon
and Maple Syrup*
ᵛ Buttermilk Pancakes with Sour Cream and Jam
*Buttermilk Pancakes with Crème Fraîche,
Dill and Smoked Salmon*
ᵛ Drop Scones

Pancakes have got me out of so many tight corners, particularly when the children were young, that I simply had to include them in this book. Often, when we used to arrive home late in the afternoon and they were tired and weary, I would whizz up some batter and within minutes would be flipping pancakes which always miraculously seemed to appease them.

Flour, milk and eggs, the ingredients for pancakes, crumpets and fritters, are virtually always to hand. All are variations on the same theme — enormously versatile, with both sweet and savoury possibilities. They really are the great convertibles.

Corn Fritters with Pangrilled Chicken Breasts and Crispy Bacon

For me corn fritters bring back memories of Chicken Maryland — one of the hottest items on trendy menus in the sixties! They still taste great, even with crispy bacon and no chicken.

4 cobs fresh sweetcorn
or 1 × 410 g tin
3 tablespoons (4 American
tablespoon) flour
½ teaspoon baking powder
2 eggs, free-range
if possible
2½ fl oz (65 ml/generous
¼ cup) milk
½ tablespoon butter, melted
1 tablespoon approx. chopped
fresh parsley
salt and freshly ground pepper

Garnish
sprigs of parsley

Accompaniment
8 Pangrilled Chicken Breasts
(see page 22)
16 rashers bacon,
fried until crisp

*Serves 8 approx. — makes 24
fritters approx.*

Scrape the kernels off the cobs into a
bowl with the back of a knife or drain
the corn kernels from the tin.

Sieve the flour and baking
powder into a bowl, make a well in
the centre and drop in the lightly
beaten eggs. Using a small whisk or
wooden spoon, stir continuously,
gradually drawing in the flour from
the sides and adding the milk in a
steady stream at the same time. When
all the flour has been incorporated,
whisk in the remainder of the milk
and the cool melted butter. Add the
corn kernels and parsley and season
with salt and freshly ground pepper.

Heat a non-stick frying pan on a
medium heat, drop a tablespoon of
the batter at a time on to the pan
leaving room for expansion. Cook
until golden brown, flip over and
cook the other side.

Serve with Pangrilled Chicken
Breasts and crispy bacon. Garnish
with sprigs of parsley and
serve immediately.

Toad in the Hole

¼ lb (110 g/scant 1 cup) flour
2 eggs, free-range if possible
½ pint (300 ml/1¼ cups) milk
½ oz (15 g/⅛ stick)
butter, melted

½ lb (225 g) best quality pork
sausages *or* cocktail sausages
(for individual toads!)
a little oil

Garnish
chopped fresh parsley

First make the batter. Sieve the flour
into a bowl, make a well in the centre
and drop in the lightly beaten eggs.
Using a small whisk or wooden
spoon, stir continuously, gradually
drawing in the flour from the sides,
and adding the milk in a steady stream

Preparation of Orzo Salad with Pesto, Cherry Tomatoes and Knockalara
Cheese

Couscous with Apricots and Toasted Almonds

Boiled Egg with Soldiers and Asparagus

Scrambled Eggs with Smoked Salmon

Preparation of Focaccia with Red Onion, Olives and Rosemary

at the same time. When all the flour has been incorporated, whisk in the remainder of the milk and the cool melted butter.

Allow to stand while you cook the sausages in a very little oil in a frying pan until pale golden on all sides.

Grease hot, deep patty tins with oil and fill ½-¾ full with the batter. Stick a cocktail sausage into each and bake in a preheated oven,

230°C/450°F/regulo 8, for 20 minutes approx.

Alternatively, pour the sausages and their cooking fat into a small roasting tin, heat on the stove for a few seconds and when it begins to sizzle pour the batter over the sausages. Bake in a pre-heated oven as described above for 20-25 minutes or until well risen and crisp. Sprinkle with chopped parsley and serve.

^v Pancakes

*P*ancakes *are far too simple and delicious to be served only on Shrove Tuesday. Whip up a batter with flour and milk and in a matter of minutes you will be flipping delicious speckled pancakes. These can be served in all sorts of ways, either savoury or sweet.*

Pancake Batter
**6 oz (170 g/generous 1 cup)
    plain white flour,
    unbleached if possible
a good pinch of salt
1 dessertspoon (8 g/2 American
    teaspoons) castor
    sugar (omit for
    savoury pancakes)
2 large eggs and 1-2 egg yolks,
    free-range if possible
scant ¾ pint (450 ml/1¼ cups)
    milk, *or* for very crisp,
    light delicate pancakes,
    milk and water mixed
3-4 dessertspoons melted butter**

**non-stick frying pan, 8 inch
(20.5 cm) diameter**

Serves 6 — makes 12 approx.

Sieve the flour, salt and sugar (if making sweet pancakes) into a bowl, make a well in the centre and drop in the lightly beaten eggs. With a whisk or wooden spoon, starting in the centre, mix the egg and gradually draw in the flour. Add the liquid slowly and beat until the batter is covered with bubbles. If the pancakes are to be served with sugar and lemon juice, stir in an extra tablespoon of castor sugar and the finely grated rind of half a lemon.

Let the batter stand in a cold place if you have time. Just before you cook the pancakes, stir in the melted butter. This will make all the difference to the flavour and texture of the pancakes and will make it possible to cook them without greasing the pan each time.

Heat a non-stick pan over a high heat, pour in a small ladleful of batter or just enough to film the base of the pan. The batter should cook

immediately. Loosen around the edges with a non-stick fish slice, flip over and cook for a few seconds on the other side. Slide on to a plate and serve with your chosen filling, either sweet or savoury.

ᵛ Savoury Herb Pancakes

Stir a few tablespoons of chopped fresh herbs into the batter and cook as above.

Suggested fillings for Savoury Herb Pancakes: Well seasoned mushrooms or Mushroom à la Crème (see page 102). Bacon, crispy pieces of chicken,

mussels, shrimps or whatever tasty bits you come across in the fridge, added to Mushroom à la Crème, make a delicious filling, as do goat's cheese, or Tomato Fondue (see page 101), or Pesto (see page 60).

ᵛ Sweet Pancakes

Suggested fillings might be:
Butter, freshly squeezed lemon juice and sugar

Sliced bananas and Toffee Sauce (see page 112)

Buttered apples laced with

mixed spices (see page 116)
Cinnamon butter
Melted chocolate and cream
Homemade jam and cream
Honey and chopped walnuts

Buttermilk Pancakes with Crispy Bacon and Maple Syrup

1 lb (450 g/3 generous cups) plain white flour
1 teaspoon bread soda
a large pinch of salt
1-2 oz (30-55 g/generous ¼ cup) sugar
1 egg, free-range if possible
1 pint (600 ml/2½ cups) buttermilk

Accompaniment
butter
20 hot crispy streaky rashers of bacon (2 per person)
maple syrup *or* Irish honey

Serves 10

Mix the dry ingredients together in a bowl, make a well in the centre, add the lightly beaten egg and enough buttermilk to make a batter of a dropping consistency (it usually takes the full pint). Drop a large tablespoonful on to a non-stick pan, and cook for 3-4 minutes on one side before turning over: the pancakes are ready to turn when the bubbles burst.

Flip over gently and cook until golden on the other side.

To serve, put one pancake on a hot plate, spread with butter and drizzle with maple syrup or honey, then top with another buttered pancake. Put a few pieces of hot crispy bacon on top. Serve more maple syrup or honey as an accompaniment.

ᵛBUTTERMILK PANCAKES WITH SOUR CREAM AND JAM

S erve the hot pancakes sandwiched together with jam and sour cream.

BUTTERMILK PANCAKES WITH CRÈME FRAÎCHE, DILL AND SMOKED SALMON

P ut a blob of crème fraîche (e.g. Jockey) mixed with chopped fresh dill on to a pancake, top with some Sweet Cucumber Salad (see below) and a few strips of smoked salmon. Garnish with a sprig of fresh dill and a couple of chives. Serve immediately.

SWEET CUCUMBER SALAD
6 oz (170 g/1 cup) approx.
 cucumber, thinly sliced
2 oz (55 g/½ cup) approx.
 onion, thinly sliced

2 oz (55 g/generous
 ¼ cup) sugar
1¼ level teaspoon salt
2½ tablespoons (35 ml/3 generous
 American tablespoons)
 white wine vinegar

Combine the cucumber and onion in a large bowl. Mix the sugar, salt and vinegar together and pour over the cucumber and onion. Place in a tightly covered container in the fridge and leave for at least 30 minutes.

ᵛDrop Scones

A *nother great stand-by, Drop Scones can be made in minutes with ingredients you probably have to hand. Cook them directly on a non-stick pan* *and eat them while they are still warm, with butter and apple jelly or a blob of cream and some fresh berries.*

8 oz (225 g/1¾ cups) white flour,
    unbleached if possible
2 oz (55 g/scant ¼ cup)
    castor sugar
¼ teaspoon salt
½ teaspoon bread soda
1 teaspoon cream of tartar
    (e.g. Bextartar)
1 oz (30 g/¼ stick) soft butter
2 eggs, free-range if possible
8 fl oz (250 ml/1 cup) milk

Makes 15 approx.

Sieve the dry ingredients into a bowl
and rub in the butter. Make a well in
the centre, drop in the lightly beaten
eggs, add a little of the milk and stir
rapidly with a whisk, allowing the
flour to be drawn in gradually
from the sides. When half the milk
is added, beat until air bubbles rise.
Add the remainder of the milk. (The
scones are usually lighter if the batter
is allowed to stand, but I often cook
them immediately with very
acceptable results!)

Drop a good dessertspoonful at a
time on to a hottish non-stick pan
and cook until bubbles appear on the
top — it usually takes a bit of trial and
error to get the temperature right.
Flip over and cook until golden on
the other side. Serve immediately.

Sandwiches
and Breads

Croissants with Ham, Mushrooms and
Melted Cheddar Cheese
Croissants with Crispy Bacon
and Roasted Red Peppers
Chicken, Avocado and Mayonnaise with Sundried
Tomatoes in a Crusty Roll
Mussels, Avocado and Mayonnaise in a Crusty Roll
v* Flat Mushroom Burgers with Pesto,
Goat's Cheese and Sundried Tomatoes
v* Crawford Café Bruschetta
* Quesadillas with Chicken and Salsa
v* Crunchy Tops
v Focaccia with Red Onion, Olives and Rosemary
v Panzerotte
v Pizzette
v French Toast with Bananas or Maple Syrup

S andwiches have been around ever since the Earl of Sandwich first slapped pieces of bread around meat to sustain him through a 24-hour session at the gaming table in 1762. Until relatively recently, though, the very word sandwich has conjured up a rather dismal picture of soggy cotton-wool sliced pan, margarine and some plastic ham or cheese.

However in the last few years a sandwich revolution has begun. Suddenly the blinkers are off and people are making wonderful sandwiches with all sorts of interesting breads and unusual fillings — croissants with various stuffings, Focaccia and Ciabatta with roast Mediterranean vegetables, pitta bread stuffed to capacity with hummus bi tahina. These have transformed the mundane image of the sandwich into something that is fashionable and fun.

This section is only a small taster to encourage you to experiment

further. There are two essentials: the quality of the bread, and great generosity when it comes to the filling.

* Croissants with Ham, Mushrooms and Melted Cheddar Cheese

4 best quality butter croissants
4 oz (110 g/2 cups)
mushrooms, sliced
extra virgin olive oil *or* **butter**
salt and freshly
ground pepper
4 slices cooked ham
or **bacon**
English mustard
4 oz (110 g/1 cup) mature
Cheddar cheese
(we use Mitchelstown),
grated

Serves 4

Put the croissants into a hot oven or under a preheated grill for a few minutes to warm and crisp.

Sauté the mushrooms in a little olive oil or butter on a hot pan for 3-4 minutes, season with salt and freshly ground pepper.

Split the croissants in half horizontally. Fill generously with mushrooms and ham, smear the ham generously with English mustard and top with grated cheese. Pop under the grill for a few minutes to melt the cheese, fold over the top and eat immediately while still hot.

* Croissants with Crispy Bacon and Roasted Red Peppers

4 best quality butter croissants
4 roasted red peppers, peeled
(see page 16)
4 teaspoons Pesto (see page 60)
4 slices Mozzarella cheese
(buffalo if possible)
4 rashers of crispy bacon

Garnish
rocket leaves
a few tiny black olives
red and yellow cherry tomatoes

Serves 4

Put the croissants into a hot oven or under a preheated grill to warm and crisp.

Split them in half horizontally. Put a few pieces of warm roasted red pepper on the base of each croissant, spread with a little Pesto, top with a slice of Mozzarella and pop under the grill until the cheese starts to soften. Smear with a little more Pesto if you are addicted, a piece of crispy bacon comes next and then put the top back on.

Serve immediately on hot plates garnished with rocket leaves and maybe a few olives and a red and yellow cherry tomato.

Chicken, Avocado and Mayonnaise with Sundried Tomatoes in a Crusty Roll

6 crispy rolls, sliced open
1-2 free-range chicken breasts,
    skinless and boneless
1 avocado, cubed
6 sundried tomatoes, chopped
salt and freshly
    ground pepper
a little extra virgin olive oil
1 tablespoon Mayonnaise
    (see page 39)
1 tablespoon approx.
    basil leaves
6 tablespoons approx.
    shredded iceberg lettuce

Garnish
rocket leaves
a few black olives
cherry tomatoes, sliced

Serves 6

Season the chicken breasts with salt and freshly ground pepper and brush with olive oil. Pangrill them until golden on both sides but still juicy and tender.

Slice into strips, mix with the avocado, sundried tomatoes, mayonnaise and torn basil leaves. Season generously with salt and freshly ground pepper and toss very gently.

Put a tablespoon of shredded iceberg lettuce into each bread roll, top with a dollop of the chicken filling and put the lid back down. Garnish with rocket leaves, a few black olives and some cherry tomato slices.

Mussels, Avocado and Mayonnaise in a Crusty Roll

6 round crusty rolls, sliced in two
2 lb (900 g) mussels
1 avocado, diced
6 tablespoons approx. shredded
    iceberg lettuce
salt and freshly ground pepper

2-3 tablespoons (2½-4 American
    tablespoons) Mayonnaise
    (see page 39) *or* Garlic
    Mayonnaise (see page 40)
1-2 tablespoons chopped
    fresh parsley

Garnish
cress *or* parsley

Serves 6

Wash the mussels and put them
into a frying pan in a single layer
(if necessary cook them in two
batches). Cover with a lid or a
folded tea towel, put on a high heat
and whip out the mussels as soon as
they open — 2-3 minutes approx.
Remove the beard and discard the
shells. Cool.

Slice the top off each roll, remove
a little of the crumb and pop into a
hot oven to crisp up if necessary.

Add the diced avocado to the
mussels. Season with salt and freshly
ground pepper, add the mayonnaise
and parsley and mix together gently.
Taste and correct the seasoning.

Put a tablespoon of shredded
iceberg lettuce on the base of each
roll, top with a generous spoonful
of the mussel mixture and put the
lid back on at an angle. Garnish with
a little cress or parsley.

^{v*} Flat Mushroom Burgers with Pesto, Goat's Cheese and Sundried Tomatoes

*Large flat mushrooms (called Portobellos
in America) are almost meaty in
texture and make a great filling for a
veggie burger.*

**6 hamburger buns *or* croûtons
    toasted or crisped in
    extra virgin olive oil
6 large flat mushrooms
salt and freshly ground pepper
extra virgin olive oil
2 cloves of garlic, crushed
2 teaspoons thyme leaves
    (optional)
6 rounds goat's cheese — St Tola
Pesto (see page 60)
a few pieces of
    sundried tomatoes**

Garnish
**a sprig of parsley
    or rocket leaves
6 cherry tomatoes**

Serves 6

Season the mushrooms well with salt
and freshly ground pepper. Arrange in
a single layer in a roasting tin, drizzle
with olive oil, sprinkle with crushed
garlic and a few thyme leaves if you
have them to hand. Cook in a hot
oven, 230°C/450°F/regulo 8, for
10-15 minutes depending on size.
Pop the hamburger buns into the
oven for a few minutes to crisp
and heat.

Top each of the mushrooms with a slice of goat's cheese, and put back into the oven or under a grill for 1-2 minutes until the cheese begins to melt. Smear the melted goat's cheese with a little Pesto and add the sundried tomato. Split the hamburger buns and make a sandwich using the hot mushroom as a filling.

Serve immediately on hot plates garnished with a little sprig of parsley or rocket leaves. Top with a cherry tomato. Take a slice off the base so that it will sit securely!

^{v*} Crawford Café Bruschetta

Bruschetta can be quite elaborate or as simple as a slice of chargrilled or toasted country bread rubbed with garlic and drizzled with extra virgin olive oil. Originally a peasant dish, it now stars on many restaurant menus. This one was created by Rory O'Connell for the Crawford Café in Cork.

1 slice country bread
1 clove of garlic
5-6 rocket leaves
roast red and yellow pepper,
    peeled and deseeded
    (see page 16 for method)
3-4 slices tomato and basil
    or marjoram salad
    (see page 10)
1-2 slices pangrilled aubergine
fresh shavings of Parmesan cheese
    (Parmigiano Reggiano
    if possible)

sea salt, freshly cracked pepper
extra virgin olive oil

Garnish
5-6 black olives, big and small
1 sundried tomato, finely sliced

Serves 1

Just before serving, chargrill or toast the bread. Put on to a plate and rub on both sides with a cut clove of garlic. Top with a few rocket leaves, two or three pieces of roast pepper, some tomato salad and a slice or two of pangrilled aubergine. Put a few slivers of Parmesan cheese on top. Sprinkle with sea salt and freshly cracked pepper.

Garnish the plate with olives and a few pieces of sundried tomato.

[*] Quesadillas with Chicken and Salsa

12 × 6-7 inch (15-18 cm) corn
    or flour tortillas
12 oz (340 g/2½ cups) cooked
    chicken meat, shredded

6-9 oz (170-255 g/1½-2¼ cups)
    grated Mozzarella *or* Cheddar
    cheese *or* a mixture
3-4 fresh green chillies,
    thinly sliced

salt and freshly ground pepper
**4-6 tablespoons (5-8 American
    tablespoons) scallion, green
    and white parts, chopped**

Accompaniments
Guacamole (see page 14)
**Tomato and Coriander Salsa
    (see page 29)**

Garnish
fresh coriander leaves
fresh chillies

Serves 6

Put a non-stick pan on a medium
heat. Place a tortilla on the pan,
sprinkle with 1-1½ oz (30-45 g) of
the grated cheese, a few slivers of
chilli, top with some chicken, season

with salt and freshly ground pepper
and a few pieces of chopped scallion.
Top with another tortilla. When the
cheese begins to melt, quickly flip
over and cook for a further minute or
so. Repeat the process with other
tortillas. Alternatively use just one
tortilla and make a turnover.

Cut each tortilla sandwich into
quarters and arrange in a line on a
warm plate. Put a blob of Guacamole
on one side and Tomato Salsa on the
other. Garnish with fresh coriander
leaves and a whole chilli. Serve
immediately.

Variation: A tablespoon of Tomato
Fondue (see page 101) added to the
tortilla along with the cheese and
chicken filling is delicious. Omit the
Tomato Salsa garnish and serve just
with Guacamole.

^{v*} Crunchy Tops

T*hese crunchy-topped scones join up
in the baking tin to make a full loaf.
Choose the topping that appeals most
to you.*

**1 lb (450 g/3 generous cups)
    white flour, unbleached
    if possible**
**1 level teaspoon (½ American
    teaspoon) breadsoda**
**1 level teaspoon (½ American
    teaspoon) salt**
**12-13 fl oz (350-370 ml/1½ cups)
    approx. buttermilk to mix**
**egg wash *or* buttermilk
    for brushing**

Topping
**seeds of your choice — sunflower
    seeds, sesame seeds, kibbled
    wheat, caraway seeds, poppy
    seeds *or* oatflakes**
**grated cheese also makes a
    delicious topping**

**1 round tin, 9 inches (23 cm)
    across × 1½ inches (4 cm)
    high, well greased with
    butter *or* olive oil**
3 inch (7½ cm) scone cutter

Makes 7

First fully preheat the oven to 230°C/450°F/regulo 8.

Sieve the dry ingredients, mix together and make a well in the centre. Pour most of the buttermilk in at once. Using one hand, mix in the flour from the sides of the bowl, adding more milk if necessary. The dough should be softish but not too wet and sticky. When it all comes together, turn it out on to a floured board and knead lightly for a second — just enough to tidy it up.

Pat the dough into a round about 1½ inches (4 cm) thick and stamp out 7 scones with the scone cutter. Brush the top of each scone with egg wash or buttermilk and dip the top in the seeds of your choice, or some grated cheese. Arrange side by side in a well greased tin.

Bake in the fully preheated oven for 25-30 minutes, or until fully cooked. If you are in doubt, tap the bottom of the bread: when it is cooked it will sound hollow. Remove from the tin and allow to cool on a wire tray.

ᵛFocaccia with Red Onion, Olives and Rosemary

P*roper' Italian Focaccia is made with a yeast bread dough, which is beyond the time limit for the recipes in this book. However, this soda bread version is irresistible and takes only minutes to make.*

White Soda Bread
1 lb (450 g/3 generous cups) white flour
1 level teaspoon (½ American teaspoon) breadsoda
1 level teaspoon (½ American teaspoon) salt
12-13 fl oz (350-375 ml/1½ cups) approx. sour milk *or* buttermilk, to mix

Topping
10-12 black olives (Niçoise *or* Kalamati)
½ red onion — 3 oz (85 g) approx.

1 tablespoon approx. chopped fresh rosemary, thyme *or* oregano
extra virgin olive oil for brushing
sea salt

Swiss roll tin, 9 × 12½ inch (23 × 31.5 cm)

Preheat the oven to 250°C/475°F/regulo 9.

Sieve the dry ingredients, mix together and make a well in the centre. Pour most of the milk in at once. Using one hand, mix in the flour from the sides of the bowl, adding more milk if necessary. The dough should be softish but not too wet and sticky. When it all comes together, turn it out on to a floured board. Brush the tin generously with the olive oil. Roll the dough quickly into a rectangle and press gently into the tin.

Brush the surface generously with olive oil, and dot with black olives and thin wedges of onion. Sprinkle with chopped rosemary, thyme or oregano and some flakes of sea salt. Bake in the fully preheated oven for 15 minutes approx. or until brown and crisp and golden on top. Brush again with a little olive oil. Cool on a wire rack and serve while still warm.

ᵛ Panzerotte

These delightful sounding packages are made with yeast bread dough in Italy, but we've had great success making them with our native white soda bread. As a result these portable bite-sized treats can be made in minutes. Use your imagination and whatever you come across in your fridge to come up with a myriad of exciting fillings. They can be baked or deep-fried.

**½ white soda bread recipe
(see page 89)
fillings of your choice e.g.
Mozzarella cheese, tomato,
basil, freshly grated
Parmesan cheese, diced
salami, pepperoni, Feta
cheese, diced smoked salmon
extra virgin olive oil *or* egg wash
for brushing**

4-inch (10 cm) cutter

Makes 6 approx.

Preheat the oven to 230°C/450°F/regulo 8, or heat a good quality oil in a deep-frier to 190°C/375°F. Make the soda bread dough in the usual way.

Roll out as thinly as possible — not more than ¼ inch (5 mm) thick. Use the cutter to stamp it into rounds.

Top with a generous tablespoon of well seasoned filling, e.g. a mixture of diced salami or pepperoni and chopped tomato and basil, well sprinkled with grated Parmesan; or a ½ oz (15 g) piece of Feta cheese, 1 teaspoon of chopped tomato, a couple of basil leaves, salt and freshly ground pepper; or diced smoked salmon, cream cheese and chopped dill.

You can vary the fillings to your heart's content, but make sure they are generous and highly seasoned. Brush the edge of each circle with cold water, fold over into a half moon shape and seal securely with your fingers or press with the tines of a fork.

Pop on to an oiled oven sheet, brush the tops with olive oil or egg wash and bake for 15 minutes approx. Alternatively slide a few at a time (unglazed) into the preheated deep-frier. Cook until golden brown — 5 minutes approx. Drain on kitchen paper and serve immediately.

^V Pizzette

½ **white soda bread recipe
(see page 89)**
pizza toppings of your choice
extra virgin olive oil

3 inch (7.5 cm) scone cutter

Makes 12

Preheat the oven to
230°C/450°F/regulo 8. Make the
soda bread dough in the usual way.

Roll out the dough as thinly as
possible — not more than ¼ inch
(5 mm) thick. Use the cutter to stamp
it into rounds, and arrange them side
by side on an oiled baking tray. Put
a generous spoonful of well seasoned

topping in the centre of each circle
of dough.

Bake in the preheated oven for
12-15 minutes. Eat immediately.

Apart from the obvious Tomato
Fondue (see page 101), Piperonata
(see page 103) or Mushroom à la
Crème (see page 102), toppings can
be as simple as a few torn basil leaves
with a blob of Mozzarella cheese.
Add anchovies or sundried tomato
if you fancy, crispy bacon, mussels,
greens (e.g. spinach leaves, rocket or
mustard greens) and Feta cheese,
golden onions, blue cheese and a
sprig of rosemary, or a dab of Pesto
(see page 60) topped with a thick
slice of tomato.

^V French Toast with Bananas and Maple Syrup or Honey

1 egg, free-range if possible
**2 tablespoons (2½ American
tablespoons) milk**
1 teaspoon sugar
1 banana
2 slices white bread
a little clarified butter (see page 72)

Garnish
1 banana
**best quality natural yoghurt,
chilled**
maple syrup *or* honey
**1 tablespoon roughly
chopped walnuts**

Serves 2

Whisk together the egg and milk in a
bowl. Add the sugar. Mash the
banana well with a fork and add to
the mixture. Alternatively whizz the
whole lot together in a liquidiser or
food processor. Pour on to a plate and
dip both sides of the bread in it.

Melt a little clarified butter in the
pan. Fry the bread on a medium heat
and when golden on one side turn
over on to the other. Put on a hot
plate. Top with sliced banana and a
blob of chilled yoghurt, drizzle
with maple syrup or honey and
scatter with a few chopped walnuts.
Serve immediately.

Salads

vv ***A Good Green Salad with Various Dressings***
vv ***Greek Green Salad***
Caesar Salad
vv ***Pineapple, Cucumber and Mint Salad***
Thai Cucumber Salad
Tuna Fish Salad

Thankfully, gone are the days when a wilted butterhead lettuce was the only thing available as the basis for a salad — which usually meant lettuce leaves with hardboiled eggs, tomatoes, a few slices of vinegary beetroot and a dollop of salad cream. Now all sorts of colourful vegetables and fruits are tumbling off the shelves of even the smallest supermarkets, making it easy for us to conjure up an infinite number of crisp and tasty combinations.

When you are in a hurry, salads can be your salvation. First, they are really fast to prepare — quicker than almost any cooked vegetable you can think of. The second point to bear in mind is that they can be a starter, an accompaniment or even a whole meal. Salads are also extremely nutritious and have the great advantage of being appetising but not too heavy.

As with so many other good fast foods, the flavour of the finished salad will depend on the quality of the ingredients. Try to grow your own vegetables and fruits if you can, or search out organically grown produce in your locality. You will have to pay more but it will be worth it — both for the taste and for the reassurance that you aren't eating a huge dose of chemicals.

I am starting, once again, with a really good green salad because it is such a great mainstay — and still surprisingly difficult to find well executed in restaurants. However, it would be a mistake to think that salad must mean green salad. There are endless other possibilities. The one constant must be a good dressing, based on best quality ingredients. Dressing isn't worth a toss unless it's made with fruity olive oil and wine vinegar.

ᵛᵛ A Good Green Salad with Various Dressings

*A*n interesting green salad makes a delicious low-calorie starter and a light and delicious accompaniment to almost every meal — except breakfast of course!

**a selection of fresh lettuces and
salad leaves — butterhead,
oakleaf, iceberg, lollo rosso,
frisée, mesculum *or* saladisi
red orach
mustard greens**

**rocket (Arugula)
tiny sprigs of fresh herbs —
parsley, dill, tarragon,
golden marjoram,
annual marjoram
or mint
a few chive flowers *or* marigold
petals if available
wild garlic — delicious
in spring if you can find it**

DRESSING

*T*he flavour of the dressing will depend on the quality of the oils and vinegars.

BASIC FRENCH DRESSING
**6 tablespoons (8 American
tablespoons) extra virgin
olive oil
2 tablespoons (2½ American**
**tablespoons) wine vinegar
sea salt and freshly
ground pepper**

Whisk all the ingredients together. Just before the salad is to be eaten, toss gently with a little dressing — just enough to make the leaves glisten.

VARIATIONS

HERB DRESSING
Add 1 tablespoonful approx. of chopped fresh herbs to the basic dressing, e.g. parsley, chives, thyme and mint.

HONEY AND HERB DRESSING
Add 1 clove of crushed garlic and a spot of honey to the herb dressing.

ANCHOVY DRESSING
Mash two anchovy fillets and add to the basic dressing with 1 teaspoonful of chopped fresh parsley and a crushed garlic clove.

CORIANDER AND GINGER DRESSING
Add 1 tablespoonful approx. of chopped fresh coriander leaves, 1 teaspoonful of finely chopped fresh ginger and 1 finely chopped spring onion to the basic dressing.

^{vv} Greek Green Salad

I ate this crisp chilled salad in a little
taverna overlooking a harbour on the
island of Aegina on a warm spring day —
so simple and quite wonderful.

**1 cos (Romaine) *or* similar
crisp lettuce
3-4 scallions *or* spring
onions, sliced
sprigs of dill
4 tablespoons approx. Greek
extra virgin olive oil
1-2 tablespoons approx. freshly
squeezed lemon juice
salt and freshly ground pepper**

Wash, drain and chill the lettuce.
Slice across the grain ¼ inch
(5 mm) thick approx. Put into a
bowl, sprinkle with sliced scallion
or spring onions and tiny sprigs of
dill. Just before serving mix the
olive oil with the lemon juice.
Sprinkle over the salad, season with
salt and freshly ground pepper, toss
and serve immediately.

Caesar Salad

T he legendary Caesar Salad has
suddenly become all the rage. It can
be made in a few minutes at home.

**1 large head of cos
(Romaine) lettuce
2 oz (55 g/½ cup) freshly grated
Parmesan cheese (Parmigiano
Reggiano if possible)
2 slices white bread, diced
into ¼ inch (5 mm) cubes
extra virgin olive oil**

Dressing
**1 × 2 oz (55 g) tin anchovies
2 egg yolks, free-range
if possible
2 tablespoons (2½ American
tablespoons) freshly
squeezed lemon juice
1 clove of garlic, crushed**

**a generous pinch of English
mustard powder
½ teaspoon salt
½-1 tablespoon Worcester sauce
½-1 tablespoon Tabasco sauce
6 fl oz (175 ml/¾ cup)
sunflower oil
2 fl oz (50 ml) extra virgin
olive oil
2 fl oz (50 ml) cold water**

Serves 4

Wash the lettuce leaves, dry really
thoroughly and chill while you make
the dressing. I make it in a food
processor but it can also be made very
quickly by hand.
  Drain the anchovies and crush
lightly with a fork. Put into a bowl
with the egg yolks, add the lemon
juice, garlic, mustard powder, salt,

Greek Green Salad ingredients

Banana Brulée

Strawberry Shortcake

Yoghurt with Honey and Toasted Hazelnuts

Balloons